the women
we wanted to look like

*the women
we wanted to look like*

Brigid Keenan

M

For Alan and Hester

Half-title page: Hedy Lamarr
Title page: Jean Shrimpton, photographed by
            David Bailey

First published 1977 by
Macmillan London Limited
Associated companies in Delhi, Dublin,
Hong Kong, Johannesburg, Lagos, Melbourne,
New York, Singapore and Tokyo

British Library Cataloguing in Publication Data

Keenan, Brigid
   The women we wanted to look like.
   1. Fashion – Biography   2. Women – Biography
   I. Title
   746.9'2'0922   TT505.A1

ISBN 0-333-21345-9

Printed in Great Britain by W. S. Cowell Ltd, Ipswich

Contents

Acknowledgments

I would like to thank Sir Cecil Beaton whose suggestions helped me begin this book, and Lady Diana Cooper, Baroness d'Erlanger, Toto Koopman, Vera Poincin, and – above all – Lee Penrose, for allowing me to probe their memories.

I must thank Sir Caspar John and John Trevelyan who found pictures for me; Vere French whose help and advice were invaluable; my colleagues Meriel McCooey, Margaret McCartney and Michael Roberts for their generous assistance; the staff of the *Sunday Times* library, especially Fred Sayer and Larry Chubb, for their patience; Eleanor Lambert and Laurie Zimmerman who helped me in New York; and Eileen Hose, Sir Cecil Beaton's secretary.

I am especially grateful to all the photographers whose work appears here, in particular to Horst, David Bailey and Harri Peccinotti.

I would like to thank my family and friends for their support – especially Sandra Hamilton who checked the manuscript and Christopher Matthew who allowed me to work in his home.

Lastly, I would like to acknowledge the great debt I owe to my sister Moira whose example showed me that so much is possible.

Beauty provoketh thieves sooner than gold
        As You Like It: Act I, Scene III

Introduction

Originally this was to be a straightforward book about fashion, but the more I contemplated hemlengths and waistlines and bust-darts and belts, the more convinced I became that it would be entertaining to write about the women who wore the clothes rather than to catalogue the inanimate garments themselves. More than that, I felt these women to be important—for inside every successful fashion look has been the person who carried it off so well that she influenced others around her. She might have been a socialite whose clothes reflected her status in the world, she may have been a mannequin or a model girl who wore particular styles because that was her job, she may have been a designer who dressed in a certain way deliberately, or a dropout whose influence was almost accidental. This book is about them all— the women we have wanted to look like.

In their heydays, many of these women's names were famous. But as the years go by they have become mere footnotes to social history, and sometimes not even that, for the world of fashion is a fickle one and well-dressed women leave no works of art for us to remember them by, only a few photographs or portraits—and those sometimes look faintly absurd when examined outside their context by new generations. I wanted to capture a little of the glamour, of the eccentricity, of the foolishness, of the fascination of these women before time blurs them.

Hundreds of people have influenced the way we have dressed and they continue to do so. Each person reading this book will have their own sources of inspiration, a magazine photograph of a model, a friend, a film star, or simply someone seen in the street. This is my own, very personal selection of the women we have wanted to look like, and because I had to draw the line somewhere, I have limited it to what I think of as modern women—in other words, those who made their names after the First World War.

When I first started as a fashion writer, I found that names of smart women often cropped up which meant nothing at all to me. I knew, though, that since fashion was to be my career it would be useful to be able to put faces to those names. Who on earth was Lee Miller, or Princess de Faucigny Lucinge, or Brenda Frazier, and what was so special about them that meant they were still being talked about so long after they made their impact? Being a kind of *Who's Who*, I hope this book will help newcomers to the business to build their pictures of past fashion stars, but much more, I hope the stories of these women will entertain and amuse everyone, and help to prove that fashion is not a remote, cold world in which only the rich can survive, but a quirky, eccentric affair, which does in the end touch us all.

1 The Best Dressed Women in the World

The first time I understood what the words 'Best-Dressed' really imply was in the mid-sixties when, as a young and nervous newcomer to fashion journalism, I was sent to cover the Italian collections in Rome. At each show there was a clutch of women sitting in the good front seats from whom I could not take my eyes. They were uniformly slim, and dressed immaculately in the kind of smooth, pastel dresses that Jacqueline Kennedy had recently made popular. They wore pale stockings on their elegant legs and gleaming patent pumps on their narrow feet. Their arms were hairless, their hands manicured and smooth, their hair thick and glossy and their faces lightly tanned and ageless. I had never seen anyone like them before—why, one of them actually changed her jewellery between the morning and afternoon shows. Later I was told that the ladies who had absorbed so much of my attention were Countess

Left: Gloria Vanderbilt was the girl who inspired the phrase 'poor little rich girl'. Her father died when she was a baby, she became the heiress to a fortune, and the victim of a widely publicised custody case fought between her mother and her aunt. She grew into the dark-eyed beauty in this picture, taken in 1940, but did not figure on the Best-Dressed list until 1962 when, so her citation went, she had developed into 'a mature and outstandingly elegant woman'.
Right: Mrs Reginald Fellowes was said to have launched more fashions than anyone else in the world. She delighted in dressing her boyish figure in clothes to make other women look foolish.

9

Crespi, Marella Agnelli and Princess Pignatelli, all of whom figured on the Best-Dressed lists of the time.

They were the first Best-Dressers I had ever encountered face to face, and I was intrigued as to how they achieved such perfection. One day I had the chance to find out, when I went back to Rome to interview Princess Pignatelli for *Nova* magazine. My four-day stay with the Princess was a revelation; she was obsessed with clothes and cosmetics and gathered beauty tips like other women collect recipes (she published them all in a beauty book not long afterwards). Princess Pignatelli was prepared to take infinite pains over her appearance: she visited the hairdresser every lunch time, exercised in a gym every other day, attended yoga classes, had massage treatments three times a week, and even plucked the hairs out of her legs with tweezers. As far as clothes went, the minimum she seemed to require each season was six new day dresses, six new cocktail dresses, two new evening dresses and a couple of coats and suits. In a drawer I counted forty-five pairs of gloves.

That kind of dedication to appearance seems to me an

Above: Before her marriage to an Italian count, Consuelo Crespi was well-known as one of the pretty American O'Connor twins used in a 1947 'Which Twin Has the Toni' advertisement. Consuelo is on the left.

Left: The long-legged and impeccable Italian Best-Dressers, Countess Crespi and Princess Pignatelli, photographed on a visit to New York in the sixties.

American or Continental trait. Britain produces women who are refined beauties, marvellous characters, or flamboyant dressers, but very few of the lean, groomed, cared-for creatures who figure on the Best-Dressed lists. Out of the seventy-eight names in the celebrated American Hall of Fame, only the Queen, Audrey Hepburn, Margot Fonteyn, and Princess Salima Aga Khan (the former model Sarah Crichton-Stuart) are English. This must have something to do with the fact that in Britain it has always been considered a little immoral for a woman to be pre-occupied with her looks, whilst on the Continent, girls are brought up believing that it is their duty to be so.

The Best-Dressed list was born, appropriately enough, in Paris in the early part of the twenties. Paris was then, as now, the fashion centre of the world, but in a very different way. In those days high fashion did not belong to everybody and good clothes were not mass-produced. Instead, all the new trends and ideas were created by the designers for a handful of rich society women who rivalled each other in smartness, snobbery and wealth. These women *were* fashion. Every bow or bead they wore was reported in the papers, and the loveliest among them were in constant demand as the subjects for glossy magazine photographs. Lesser mortals could only look on in awe, or, more practically, cut out the pictures and take them round the corner to their own little dressmakers. From all over the world fashionable women came to Paris to order their clothes from the great designers, and it was the designers who invented the Best-Dressed list. It started as a poll they took among themselves to decide who among their clients were the most elegant. The annual list became a favourite newspaper story, one that endured and interested readers for decades. In the early thirties, the *New York Times* reported that to be on the list meant 'a candidate must do more than invest the sum of $50,000 with the Paris dressmaking trade. She must have brains, poise and vivacity.'

The favourite name on the early lists was that of Mrs Reginald Fellowes. She undoubtedly had all those qualities. Mrs Fellowes became a legend: not because she was a writer, not because she was once Paris editor of *Harper's Bazaar*, but simply because she wore clothes better than anyone else. Her arrival at the dress shows when she was Paris editor of *Harper's* does not exactly tally with that of a working girl—she appeared wearing pristine white gloves and carrying a long-stemmed rose.

The twenties were years of extraordinary extravagance and high living. Toto Koopman, who was then a mannequin at Chanel, says, 'It was like another world. For instance, people always dressed in the evenings. If you were working like me you would rush home, bathe and then dress yourself up—and I really *mean* dress up—in lace, jewels, all sorts of hats, you had to have so many hats then. I remember my favourite was a little skull cap with two diamond clips. And gloves, one always wore gloves. Everyone went out in the evenings, there was always an In place to be seen at. We were all exhibitionists, show-offs. One dressed up not to please men, but to astound the other women.'

Mrs Reginald Fellowes was said (by Jean Cocteau) to have launched more fashions than any woman in the world. She was flat-chested, sleek and slim with a neat glossy head (she wore her hair cut boyishly short or scraped back into a knot). She was the granddaughter of Isaac Singer, the American sewing machine king, and was enormously rich. Her first husband had been Prince Jean de Broglie, a member of one of the old families of France, but he was killed in the First World War and she married Reginald Fellowes, son of the second Lord de Ramsey. Daisy Fellowes dressed at Chanel in the twenties, but in the thirties she switched her allegiance to the outrageous Italian designer Schiaparelli, whose wildest excesses she could carry off with elegance. It was said that though she could well afford to buy Schiaparelli's business lock, stock and barrel, she dressed there free because it pleased her vanity to think that the most talked-about designer in the world would clothe her simply for prestige.

Daisy Fellowes cared not a damn what people thought of her and she would go out of her way to make other women look foolish. 'I was terrified of her' says Toto Koopman. 'She was sharp as a razor; you never knew where you stood with her.' When she was sure other women would be dressed up to the nines, Mrs Fellowes would perversely choose the simplest linen frock; if the others were in floating tea gowns she would turn up in leopardskin-printed pyjamas. She went to the races bare-headed, knowing that this would make the ladies in exuberant picture hats look absurd, and one of her more dashing garments was a sequin coat cut exactly like a man's dinner jacket.

Princess Natalie Paley (left in 1932) was considered to be the prettiest woman in Paris. She had a haunting waif-like look that photographers of the day found irresistable. *Right:* Marie-Laure de Noailles was a poet, and the intellectuals' favourite beauty. She was proud that her hands were supposed to be the smallest in Paris.

Antoine, the great hairdresser of the time, said of her, 'She liked above everything in the world to be amused. For a dinner party she would select people who detested each other and carefully seat them so that each was paired with his particular enemy—a wife and an ex-wife, a man's wife and his mistress, a writer and the critic who had torn him to pieces. At the end of the evening the hostess was charmed to see how many conflicts were in progress.'

The Duff Coopers were invited by Mrs Fellowes to cruise in the Mediterranean on her yacht. For some reason they had to cut their holiday short. 'You've done very well to last as long as this,' remarked Mrs Fellowes when she said goodbye. 'Most of my friends send themselves urgent telegrams after ten days.'

The long-waisted, short-skirted clothes of the twenties suited Phyllis de Janzé's feline figure so well that 'one did not know if it was she who had invented them, or they that had invented her', as Cecil Beaton remarked. Before her marriage to the Vicomte de Janzé in 1922 she had been Phyllis Boyd, described by her contemporaries in England as having a face like a puma with Egyptian-scarab eyes and hair as sleek as nut-brown satin. For a time she lived in Paris, where she worked for couturier Jean Patou and was so ultra-stylish and chic that she became known as the best-dressed woman in France. She is said to have been one of the very first women to wear the short skirts of the period, and she did so uninhibitedly, teaming them with extraordinary high-heeled red shoes with ankle straps. Later she abandoned Paris, her husband and her smart life and settled in London where, always surrounded by lovers or admirers, she lived a leisurely life reading and working on what Diana Cooper called 'strange freehand embroidery', interrupted only by travels to unlikely parts of the world.

Perhaps the prettiest woman in Paris in the twenties was Princess Natalie Paley. 'Her eyes are star-bright', said Cecil Beaton, who called her the most significant beauty after Garbo, 'and her laughter tinkles like a mountain stream over pebbles.' Princess Paley was the daughter of Grand Duke Paul and his second wife. The Tsar had so frowned on this marriage that the Grand Duke was banished from Russia; and like so many of her compatriots, Natalie Paley found her home in Paris. She married the French fashion designer Lucien Lelong, and her wistful, almost tragic face with its high cheekbones made her a favourite subject of the top photographers. Later she ventured into film-making—she had a part in Alexander Korda's *The Love Life of Don Juan*.

The ivory-skinned, dark-haired Vicomtesse Marie-Laure de Noailles was the intellectuals' favourite beauty. She was a poet and a patron of the arts, but appeared on early Best-Dressed lists and was proud of the fact that she had the smallest hands in Paris. She once donated a pair of gloves for a charity auction at the Paris Opera. Antoine, her hairdresser, bought one for 5,000 francs: 'She had the capacity of exciting people to such almost childish actions,' he said later, perhaps a little regretfully.

Millicent Rogers, the daughter of an American oil tycoon, loved dressing up so much that she would find excuses to change her clothes several times in an evening.

By 1935 the *New York Times* was reporting that 'half the best-dressed women in the world are Americans.' In the twenties and thirties travelling was laborious and time-consuming, yet high society was surprisingly international, and many Americans, undeterred by the long journey by ship and boat-train to the steaming station of Gare St Lazare, came to Paris to buy their clothes. Millicent Rogers was one of the well-known American beauties whose name often appeared on the Best-Dressed lists. She was the uninhibited daughter of an oil tycoon. She led a giddy social life and liked to indulge her passion for dressing up. Diana Vreeland, the famous editor of American *Vogue* recalls a ball in New York at which Millicent Rogers caused a sensation by finding excuses to change her dress several times during the evening. Toto Koopman remembers her in the Tyrolean clothes from Lanz's shop in Vienna that became a rage in the thirties. Later in the decade Miss Rogers defected from Europe and chose instead to have everything made for her by the eccentric American designer Charles James, from whom she ordered vast quantities of things—four dozen identical blouses, for instance. She presented all her Charles James clothes to the Brooklyn Museum in 1949.

A less tempestuous beauty of the period was Mrs Harrison Williams. She had short, silvery hair and pale blue eyes and dressed for maximum effect in soft and feminine dresses in pastel

Left: Mona Harrison Williams began featuring on the Best-Dressed lists at the end of the twenties. Hers was a quiet elegance that owed a good deal to immaculate grooming and to the way she enhanced her silvery hair by always dressing in pastel colours. *Right*: Mrs Simpson, photographed on the day of her marriage to the Duke of Windsor in 1937. The blue-grey crepe dress she wore was designed by Mainbocher and was the most copied garment of its year.

colours—a habit which earned her a reputation as a fashion leader in the late twenties and which has lasted until the present day. Cecil Beaton described her as a work of art, and her houses, her furniture, her jewellery and her way of life as a *tour de force*. 'More than any other woman,' he said, 'Mrs Harrison Williams possesses the American quality of freshness. No French or South American hostess could possibly have rivalled the almost unreal perfection of crispness and newness that she created in the surroundings of her Fifth Avenue house. Both mistress and mansion seemed to have just stepped out of a bandbox.'

In 1935 the name that was to shake the throne of England appeared on the Best-Dressed lists for the first time: Mrs Ernest Simpson. Every diarist and biographer of the period has noted down his or her impressions on meeting the woman for whom a king abdicated. Cecil Beaton wrote, 'Hers is the figure that is admired now . . . her taste in clothes shows always a preference for bold simplicity. Her hair, like a Japanese lady's hair, is brushed so that a fly would slip off it.' The diarist Chips Channon called her 'a jolly, plain, intelligent, quiet, unpretentious and unprepossessing little woman'. Lady Furness remembers 'she did not have the chic she has since cultivated.' Harold Nicolson described her as 'bejewelled, eyebrow-plucked, virtuous and wise'.

Mrs Simpson was a perfectionist. Antoine, who did her hair for her wedding (and admits to snipping off a lock and keeping it as a souvenir) tells how hard she worked at her appearance and surroundings. 'She had her hair dressed three times a day; in the morning for a little hat, something quite simple; in the afternoon perhaps to go to the races; in the evening for formal use, perhaps with a little ornament. This does not mean the ordinary woman's several-times-a-day-haircomb. It means a complete hairdressing by a coiffeur or a maid. Each hairdo might require half an hour.' He adds, 'Like all the world's fashion leaders, she handles her appearance and dress as though they were a business in themselves.' Antoine goes on to describe how the Duchess set about decorating her home in Nassau when the Duke was Governor of the Bahamas. 'Plainly she regarded the house as a background for herself, as every clever woman does. When it came to painting the walls of the rooms which she was to use most often this is how she chose their colour. First they were painted a dead white. When this had dried she came in with a box of her face powder and a puff. With this she patted a bit of the powder on one patch. This was to be the colour of the walls.' Frances Donaldson, in her biography of Edward VIII considered that 'her pre-occupation with her appearance, her jewellery and her clothes was unsuitable to the role of Governor's wife on a small group of islands.'

The dress Wallis Simpson wore for her wedding to the Duke of Windsor in 1937 was in a pale blue-grey crepe, long and narrow, and designed by her favourite couturier, Mainbocher. In spite of what the Editor-in-Chief of *Vogue* thought about it —'candidly, for such an occasion as her wedding to a former

Despite her pretty pink-and-white complexion and enormous blue eyes, Mrs Dudley Ward liked to emphasize her boyish figure by wearing her hair short and dressing in mannish suits.

English king, I think she and Mainbocher might have done better than they did'—pictures of the Windsor wedding appeared in papers across the globe, and the dress became the most copied garment of the year. (The original now belongs to the Costume Institute of the Metropolitan Museum, New York.)

Mrs Dudley Ward, the woman who had been the Prince of Wales's favourite for nineteen years until he fell in love with Mrs Simpson, was a fashion leader too. If Mrs Simpson had a typical thirties look, Mrs Dudley Ward was the type we associate with the twenties. She was tiny, flat-chested, with shingled hair, and had a boyish appeal which she played up to by wearing natty checked suits, often with a carnation in the buttonhole. According to Cecil Beaton, Mrs Dudley Ward had 'a million imitators . . . especially in America has her influence been an indelible one, and the idiom has become part of the American woman's personality. The juvenile grandmother . . . the baby bow in the bobbed henna hair—all are travesties of this most original little figure.'

The woman who became Queen of England because of Mrs Simpson also had her fashion triumph. George VI's shy, sweet-looking Elizabeth (now the Queen Mother) was dressed by Norman Hartnell. 'When I was first asked to design for her I didn't think it would be easy, she was small and plump. I went to the Palace rather nervously, but the King led me off to see some Winterhalter portraits and said, "I think these dresses would suit my wife, don't you?" That is how we arrived at her crinolines and off-the-shoulder necklines.'

In 1938, the year after the Windsor wedding, the King and Queen of England went on a state visit to France. The court was in mourning, and since white is the Royal alternative to black, Norman Hartnell made the Queen an all-white wardrobe. It stunned even Paris. 'Everything she took,' says Hartnell, 'was white or silver, even her shoes. I was flattered when I heard that Dior, years later, told some British press people, "When I want to think of beautiful dresses I remember the ones your Norman Hartnell did for the Queen's visit to Paris".' In Toto Koopman's eyes 'the Queen looked dazzling, simply divine. She made everyone want to wear white.'

The Royal who came nearest to having the *Parisienne* kind of chic was Princess Marina of Greece, who married the Duke of Kent in 1934. She had a crooked smile, a great deal of charm and conquered all hearts in Britain. Her clothes, hats and hair style were greatly admired and copied. In particular the blue/green colour she favoured became very popular and was known as Marina blue. Only once did 'the Princess from over the sea', as she was referred to by the newspapers, make a wrong move, and that was at George V's Jubilee celebrations, when she annoyed her father-in-law by wearing a huge cartwheel hat that obscured her face. It is an unwritten royal rule that the public should at all times have an unobstructed view of their first family.

When the Second World War engulfed Europe, the French dressmakers abandoned their Best-Dressed list. The American couturiers took it on, and published their first selection of elegant ladies in 1940. Later, Eleanor Lambert, a well-known fashion publicist in New York, undertook to compile the list herself. Every year she sends out 3,500 ballot sheets to American fashion editors, designers and celebrities, and a committee of fashion experts judges the results.

The list became rather boring after a time, because the same familiar names topped it every year. Ms Lambert found a way out, and in 1959 she invented a 'Hall of Fame' in which the absolutely faultless women of fashion would be permanently enshrined, leaving the year-to-year list open for new blood. The first four women elected to the so-called Hall of Fame were the Duchess of Windsor, Mrs William Paley, Countess Edward von Bismark (once Mrs Harrison Williams) and Queen Elizabeth II, who in 1951 had caused something of a sensation when she wore a circular felt square-dancing skirt one informal evening during a state visit to Ottawa. The Queen is not usually noted for trend-setting, but then she doesn't often wear clothes with such broad and instant appeal as that skirt. Everyone wanted one, and they were worn with waist-cinching belts and off-the-shoulder sweaters. I remember my elder sister who was a dab hand with a needle, setting up in business most successfully making felt skirts for her girl friends.

By the end of the fifties the Best-Dressed list was not the sole arbiter of elegance. John Fairchild had transformed his family's long-established trade paper, *Women's Wear Daily*, into a

Left: Queen Elizabeth photographed in an off-guard moment in Paris during the State Visit of 1938. Her dazzling-white wardrobe combined with her shy charm conquered even the capital of fashion. *Below:* Princess Marina of Greece became the Duchess of Kent in 1934. She was one of the few British women to be elected to the American Hall of Fame—fashion's equivalent of winning an Oscar.

gossipy, opinionated, often vicious but always readable source of information on who-was-who and what-was-what in the fashion business. *WWD* became a must on the subscription list of anyone who pretended to be in the know. The paper coined absurd nicknames to describe the fashion status of their favourite women. The Duchess of Windsor and Mrs Paul Mellon became 'The Impeccables'; Mrs William Paley and Mrs Loel Guinness became 'Goddesses' (Mrs Guinness is also known as 'The Ultimate'); Jaqueline Kennedy became 'Her Elegance'.

Mrs Kennedy's clothing first hit the headlines in 1960. It was the time of the election between Kennedy and Nixon and when the American press revealed that Senator Kennedy's wife had spent no less than $30,000 on clothes in Paris, it became an election issue. (To be scrupulously fair I should say that this sum was spent by both Mrs Kennedy and her mother-in-law.) Nixon supporters lost no time in publicising Mrs Nixon as a lovable, homely character in a simple cloth coat, compared to the dizzily extravagant, frivolous Mrs Kennedy.

John Kennedy became President despite his wife's apparent expensive taste in clothes, but the result of the uproar in the press was that Mrs Kennedy had to give up buying clothes in Paris for a time and choose an American designer instead. She chose Oleg Cassini and made him famous. But no matter who designed for Jacqueline Kennedy, she retained her own style: bone-simple little dresses and coats in pale colours and flat fabrics, low-heeled pumps, a bouffant bob (looked after by hairdresser Kenneth, who also became well-known under her patronage) and a pill-box hat. In the early part of the sixties, women all over the world imitated the neat Jackie Kennedy look. She had fans like a film star.

By contrast, hardly anyone knows what 'The Impeccable' Mrs Paul Mellon looks like. She leads a discreet and quiet life, in spite of being one of the richest women in America. This is what it takes to become an 'Impeccable'—Mrs Mellon used to dress at Balenciaga, but since his death she wears only Givenchy clothes. It is said that in Paris, Givenchy has to devote a whole *atelier*, or sewing room, exclusively to Mrs Mellon. There they make every stitch she wears, including her lingerie and gardening clothes. It seems she is also a perfectionist at home. In her Virginia mansion, apples are kept boiling on the stove so that the rooms are always filled with a good country smell. In her New York house there are fake shadows painted on the floors to give the impression that sun streams constantly through the windows.

'Goddess' Mrs William Paley, otherwise known as 'Babe', has been considered a fashion leader for years. She was one of the three beautiful Cushing sisters from Boston. Before the Second World War, while she worked on *Vogue*, she was described by a colleague as having thick dark hair, gazelle's eyes, a high broken nose, and, rather curiously, 'the tight high buttocks of island women who have carried things on their heads all their lives'. She is past middle-age now, her hair has

Gloria Guinness is nicknamed 'The Ultimate' because of the faultless way in which she carries off her clothes. Before the War, in Paris when she was poor, she could still outshine the fashionable ladies of the day in a simple black cardigan and skirt.

turned grey, but she still takes a size six or eight in clothes though she is over five feet eight inches tall. Mrs Paley claims that neatness and grooming are the secret of best dressing.

Gloria Guinness, known as 'The Ultimate', came from Mexico to Paris before the Second World War and her dark beauty soon had the town at her feet. John Fairchild says that even in a black cardigan and skirt she outshone the great ladies of the day—'Gloria was ahead of Paris, she always has been.' 'Years ago when I was poor,' she says, 'I would buy a beautiful piece of jersey, cut a hole in the top and put it over my head and tie a beautiful sash around my waist. Everyone asked where I bought my dresses.' In later, better days, it was reported that Mrs Guinness could not wear a glove on her right hand because her ring was too big. Gloria Guinness has been married several times, eventually to Loel Guinness, a man wealthy enough to keep her in diamonds, a yacht, several houses in pleasing places, a helicopter, and a private plane which she decorated with Louis XVI antiques.

In my own, personal Best-Dressed list I would find a place for Clare Rendlesham who runs the Saint Laurent Rive Gauche shops in London. She is English, but gifted with that chic that has always seemed the prerogative of other nationalities. She has never been mentioned on any official list—I can't imagine why, for she takes clothes more seriously than anyone else I know, dieting herself down to skin and bone to do them justice. (Given half a chance she will try to do the same for overweight guests—in a restaurant once she allowed me to eat only a raw tomato and a sliver of ham.)

If the Englishwoman still does not understand clothes, it is not because Clare Rendlesham hasn't tried to educate her. As *Young Idea* editor of *Vogue* in the sixties she encouraged and nurtured the new designers as devotedly as a mother. Mary Quant says that she would never have got off the ground without her. And in her shops she bullies the customers so ruthlessly that they have been known to check that she is out before venturing in to spend their money.

Back in the glittering, chic days of Paris in the twenties, women tried desperately to be individual, to make entrances that had their audience gasping. Daisy Fellowes once found herself wearing the same black tulle dress trimmed with ostrich feathers as a rival. Without turning a hair she grabbed some scissors, snipped the feathers off, and held them in her hand like a fan. Again, determined to be different she went to Buckingham Palace wearing a short, black jet dress with black ostrich feathers, instead of the white or pastel shades that were compulsory Court dress. She had managed to discover that a distant relative had died, which meant that she could legitimately attend the court in mourning. In recent years, this passion to be different no longer seems to possess the Best-Dressed. In the mid-sixties an Italian designer, Emilio Pucci, started producing his own unmistakable printed silk shirts and dresses. These broke out like a plague on the backs of

Below: Jacqueline Kennedy in 1962 at the height of her influence on fashion. Women all over the world copied her simple gabardine dresses, her low-heeled pumps and her bouffant hairdo topped by a pillbox hat. *Right:* Mrs William Paley (here photographed in 1934) has long been a fashion leader. 'She does not follow trends,' said *Women's Wear Daily*, 'she inspires them. She can wear a caftan to a museum opening; others follow.'

all the most fashionable women. They positively revelled in being seen wearing the same clothes, because it proved they knew what was what. Nowadays, far from keeping their sources a secret, well-dressed women wear a whole host of things stamped and printed with the initials of the designers— Gucci, Dior, Hermes, Yves Saint Laurent. It is tantamount to leaving the price ticket on—no one could make the mistake of thinking you have dressed on the cheap. Does it mean that these days the Best-Dressed are as insecure as everyone else?

The exclusive, extravagant world of the twenties vanished long ago, and as society has become more and more democratic the influence of the elegant women in the Best-Dressed lists has dwindled. More fashions are born in the streets than on the backs of the rich and famous few. In a world in which blue jeans are the best sellers, the list has lost its relevance. Nowadays newspapers are likely to give more space to the annual list of the World's *Worst*-Dressed Women.

Left: Although her clothes do not usually inspire a mass of imitators, this circular felt square-dancing skirt worn by the Queen on a visit to Ottawa was easy to copy, and became a positive craze in the fifties. *Right:* Lady Clare Rendlesham (here in 1971) has never been on a Best-Dressed list, despite being an elegant woman who takes her clothes very seriously.

2 The Great Hostesses

When the wealthy and powerful entertain they seem to practise the art of keeping-up-with-the-Joneses just as earnestly as humbler people, vying with each other to see who can lure the most brilliant intellectuals, the most glittering aristocrats, provide the most sumptuous feasts or original surroundings. Hospitable gestures like chartering aeroplanes to ferry guests to and fro, or flying in thousands of out-of-season carnations to decorate the ballroom become positively commonplace when compared with some efforts. In the thirties, for instance, Baron de Gunzberg transported flocks of beribboned sheep, whole haystacks, and farm carts full of daisies to an island in the Seine to give his outdoor picnic a nice rural touch. Elsa Maxwell broke the ice most successfully at one of her parties by installing an imitation cow and making her sophisticated friends milk it for champagne. One might imagine that since the war extravagance of this sort has died out, but not at all. When the Schlumbergers gave a ball in Portugal in 1968 they sent planes up to spray the sky with dry ice and ensure that the night would be clear and moonlit. And only recently the House of Dior made fountains flow with a new scent when they held a party to celebrate its launching.

Since the early part of the century the International Set have trailed their finery around to parties in London, Paris, Venice, Sicily and Acapulco, pursued by dogged gossip columnists who stop at nothing to see how the other half enjoys itself. I worked on the *Daily Express* years ago when tycoon Paul Getty threw a lavish, but very private party to which no reporters were invited. Undaunted, our gossip columnists talked of hiring a boat in which, with faces blackened for camouflage, they were to paddle silently down a stream and into Mr Getty's back garden. They also had invitations forged in case the first plan looked like failing. Like all social habits, entertaining has had a bearing on the clothes we wear. The cocktail dress did not exist until the cocktail party was invented, the short evening dress was dreamed up in the twenties for the new fun of night-clubbing, and the dinner dress was made for dinner parties. And it is impossible not to notice that since money has grown tighter and entertainment (with some exceptions) less lavish, evening clothes have become so informal that one hardly recognizes them as such.

The twenties was the decade that broke all the pompous rules which previously governed entertaining. The war years of unhappiness and pent-up tension were over and relief exploded

Guests at Baron de Gunzberg's fabulous costume ball in Paris in the thirties. From the left, Horst, Madame Georges Auric, Prince Jean-Louis de Faucingy Lucinge, Coco Chanel, the great fashion designer, and an unknown party-goer.

29

like fireworks. Not for nothing were they known as The Roaring Twenties. Everyone went a little crazy—they kicked their legs up doing the Charleston, they sipped cocktails for the first time, they danced cheek to cheek in nightclubs. They were jazz-mad, party-mad, and like exuberant children, enjoyed dressing up and playing pranks. This was no time for formality—the zanier the party the more energetically they threw themselves into it. Scavenger hunts became a craze. After a dinner party the guests would be paired off and sent away with a list of peculiar items they had to collect. The Bright Young Things would set off in full cry, and the first to bring back the whole list was the winner. Diana Cooper wrote, 'Treasure hunts were dangerous and scandalous but there was no sport to touch them.'

At a party in Paris to which all the *beau monde* was invited, including Mrs Reginald Fellowes, the Marquesa de Casa Maury, and Lady Mendl, the list of objects the guests had to find included:

the pom-pom from a sailor's hat
the cleverest man in Paris
a red bicycle lamp obtained in the boulevards
Baron Maurice de Rothschild's handkerchief
an autographed portrait of royalty signed that night
a swan from the Bois de Boulogne
a shoe worn by Mistinguett the actress

Lady Mendl won, but some items had to be missed out: the Baron de Rothschild was unfortunately not at home and his valet refused to part with a handkerchief, and no one could persuade the cleverest man in Paris to join in the fun. At a similar party in London the list included 'something unique': a proud guest brought back a corset belonging to Rosa Lewis of the Cavendish Hotel which had been signed by all her noble patrons.

Bottle parties, supposedly invented by Loelia Ponsonby, who later became Duchess of Westminster, originated in the twenties, but in those early days guests brought only champagne, or food, or music, or were prepared to do some entertaining themselves—literally to sing for their supper.

Freak parties became all the rage, too. It might be a Pyjama Party, or a Circus Party—at which there would probably be the extra thrill of real bears or ponies—or it might be a Come-as-You-Would-Like-to-Be Party. The guests at one of these scandalized the prudish when it was reported that most of the women came dressed as men and most of the men as women. A popular idea was the Baby Party at which guests would be trundled around in prams and play with hoops or trains.

Many of the Bright Young Things seem to have behaved pretty childishly—even when their hosts did not specify that they should—and their wild behaviour was often rebuked in the newspapers. By 1931 Chelsea residents were up in arms: 'There is much resentment among artists of this quarter against certain

From the mid-twenties Lady Mendl channelled her endless drive into hostessing, and her parties were famous. She was the first woman to tint her white hair blue.

wealthy young people from other parts who have recently rented studios to give parties.' This article complained of 'scantily attired women indulging in horse-play in the street'.

By the mid-thirties the Bright Young Things—older and wiser now—had sobered up, and only once again, in the fifties, did we catch an echo of those high-spirited goings-on, perhaps because it was another post-war decade. A party given on the Inner Circle tube line in London in 1959 was attended by debutantes and their young men and was condemned as a 'disgraceful orgy' by the press, who called them 'young people with large wallets and small brains', and went on to describe their antisocial behaviour: 'They lay on the floor, they stood on the seats, they crushed, jostled, embarrassed and spilled cheap wine over decent members of the public.' A river-boat party attended by the same crowd of young people got quite riotous and out of hand. Some people were pushed overboard, and questions were asked in the House of Commons because a member of the Royal family, the Duke of Kent, had been among the guests. The fifties even saw a revival of the Circus party, and this one was attended by a cobra, two cheetahs and the retired tiger-hunting elephant of the Maharajah of Cooch Behar.

Of all the entertainments that became popular in the twenties, the costume balls were perhaps the most spectacular. Cecil Beaton's first assignment was to cover Baroness d'Erlanger's ball in Venice in 1924. He went along nervously with two women reporters and was rather snubbed by the beauties he tried to photograph, though Baroness d'Erlanger's daughter, the well-known Baba de Faucigny Lucinge grudgingly allowed him to take a picture of her dressed as 'Water', in hundreds of strips of tin with a helmet of sequins. Diana Cooper went to the same ball dressed as a porcelain shepherdess, but was not allowed in as the Government had recently introduced a law forbidding the wearing of masks. Lady Diana had to go home and improvise another costume. Just before the d'Erlanger's party, another costume ball was given in Venice by Count Volpi for Crown Prince Umberto and the two events were neatly timed so that the international guests could attend both. Antoine, the hairdresser of the time, went to Venice to do his clients' hair for these parties. It was while coiffing ladies for costume balls that Antoine invented hair lacquer—he had to find a fixative for the complicated creations he designed. But he later said of his invention, 'This is a discovery which I almost regret because it is now so overdone and so abused. Lacquer is for evening, for formal use. In the daytime wind should blow through the hair.'

Even at the most lavish entertainments disasters frequently occurred, and in Venice Antoine was called upon at the last minute to improvise for guests whose costumes had got mislaid in the journey, or who felt they didn't look right. For an Italian admiral's wife he fixed up a harem outfit from a silver lamé piano cover, some old lace and a curtain; and when Lady Mendl lost her baggage and arrived with only her jewel box Antoine made her a turban out of a pair of black silk stockings and dressed her in his own black satin cloak which he decorated with her brooches.

The women took their dressing-up very seriously, although even Antoine apparently was surprised at the lengths to which one guest went. She appeared as the reproduction of a painting —which involved making her entrance accompanied by two rhinos hired from Venice zoo and heavily doped so as not to frighten the other guests. Diana Cooper describes the fever that possessed them all: 'More ambitious grew the *Entrées*. Greyhounds had to be hired for Artemis, pigs to be scrubbed and gold-leashed for Circe, doves to be caught and manacled for Peace, a horn for the Unicorn, and a bewildered owl for Athene's shoulder.'

At a costume ball given outside Paris just before the Second World War, Chanel (dressed as a Tree Fern) danced with her enemy Schiaparelli (dressed as Queen of the Ants) and neatly steered her into the candelabra so that Schiaparelli's antennae caught fire. The very last ball before the war was given by Lady Mendl: it was another circus party and, giant whip in hand, Lady Mendl played ringmaster to trained ponies.

There were many ways of gaining a reputation as a great hostess. It could be done by paying such faultless attention to their needs that your guests wallowed in comfort, or by ruthlessly collecting only the sharpest wits and the most brilliant brains. Elsa Maxwell, with her flair for ideas and astonishing energy, got there by simply making her parties fun. Some achieved it because they specialized: Lady Londonderry collected politicians, while Lady Ottoline Morell held court over the great writers and poets of her age. If you were desperate, you could always bribe your guests to come. Mrs Laura Corrigan arrived in London from America in the late twenties. She was enormously rich, very naive, and desperate to know all the right people. No one, however, accepted her invitations until she announced that she would be giving her guests prizes—then they flocked to her door; and the most important were rewarded with gold cigarette boxes and other expensive baubles. She once hired a palazzo in Venice and invited all her friends to visit her there. Diana Cooper was persuaded to go, and on her birthday was astonished to find that Mrs Corrigan had piled her plate high with presents. Seeing her luck, other guests unashamedly pretended that they all had birthdays coming up soon, but Mrs Corrigan did not seem to mind—at least they were there, and the only thing she demanded of them was that they posed for photographs, perhaps to prove it.

American women have always excelled at being the type of hostesses who put their guests' comfort first. Before the last war Lady Diana Cooper stayed with Mr and Mrs William Paley in their house on Long Island and wrote: 'The standard is unattainable to us tradition-ridden, tired Europeans. There was nothing ugly, worn, or makeshift; brief and exquisite meals, a little first-class wine, one snorting cocktail. Servants were invisible yet one was always tended. A little table in your bedroom was laid as for a nuptial night, with fine lawn, plates, forks and a pyramid of choice-bloomed peaches, figs, and grapes. In the bathroom were all the aids to sleep, masks for open eyes, soothing unguents and potions. In the morning a young silent girl more lovely than the sun that blazed through the hangings smoothed all and was never seen again.'

Pauline de Rothschild, an American model who in 1954 married the owner of the Mouton Rothschild vineyards in France, had a formidable reputation as the most conscientious hostess. Her guests' sheets and pillows were ironed—on the bed —every time they'd been touched, and legend had it that if a guest fell asleep with her hand hanging over the edge of the bed she would wake in the morning to find it manicured. Pauline de Rothschild scented her rooms with perfumed candles and insisted on decorating her tables only with bouquets of carefully gathered wild flowers.

Elsie de Wolfe had been a famous interior designer in America but after her late marriage in 1926 to an English aristocrat she dedicated her considerable energies to hostessing in her chateau at Versailles. Lady Mendl devoted a whole filing system to her guests—there she could see at a glance how many times so-and-so had been before, what he had eaten, whom he had met and even what table decorations he had seen. Cecil Beaton recalls her 'fetishistic concern for trivialities' and describes how she bullied her immaculately-trained servants: 'If a hot cheese biscuit was served with the wrong dish, or a cocktail was insufficiently shaken, there would more than likely be a court martial.' Lady Mendl was equally fastidious about her own appearance and dressed with understated smartness first at Chanel, then at Mainbocher. 'She convinced a great many women that her way was the only way to dress,' said Bettina Ballard, the *Vogue* Paris correspondent of those days, and described Lady Mendl's Wednesday afternoon At Homes as 'parade grounds for fashion'. Lady Mendl was no beauty, though her looks improved with age and, it is said, with facial surgery. Probably she was best known for being the very first woman to dye her white hair pale blue. She created such a rage for it that Antoine her hairdresser had to have no less than twelve different shades of blue made up for his clients. He arrived at Lady Mendl's colour by a system of trial and error, testing the various hues on his white Russian Borzoi dog, Da.

When Cecil Beaton described Emerald Cunard as a hostess in his first book it enraged her so much that she burned her copy in front of the luncheon guests. A good many of the hostesses of the day were rather stupid and Emerald Cunard could not bear to be classed with women like Lady Colefax, who, it is said, invited Einstein to lunch and then could not think of anything to talk to him about. She is supposed to have turned to the great man with the words, 'Bogie says Philip is ruining Charlie'—an idiotic piece of London gossip which must have baffled the refugee newly arrived from Germany.

Baroness Pauline de Rothschild had been a model at Hattie Carnegie's in New York. She had a tremendous sense of style which, after her marriage to Baron de Rothschild, she applied to the art of hostessing.

Emerald Cunard gained the reputation of being the greatest hostess of them all. In old age she lived at the Dorchester Hotel but continued to invite guests, though her rooms were so small that the waiters found it almost impossible to manoeuvre around the dinner table.

Lady Cunard belonged to the category of hostesses who collected brilliant people. She was American, but in New York had met and married Sir Bache Cunard, the fox-hunting grandson of the founder of the shipping line. After her marriage she found herself suffocating with boredom in his country house in Leicestershire, and in 1911 she left him and came to London. There she became perhaps the best-known hostess of all. 'It was in her house at Grosvenor Square,' wrote Chips Channon, 'that the great met the gay, that statesmen consorted with society, and writers with the rich. . . . It was a rallying point for most of London society: only those that were too stupid to amuse the hostess, and so were not invited, were disdainful.'

Lady Cunard's first name was Maud but she was better known as Emerald 'the jewels I wear are emeralds and since I am nicknamed the Emerald Queen, I have adopted it as my Christian name.' She was a tiny blonde woman with rouged cheeks and her contemporaries always described her as though she were a bird: 'like a yellow canary', 'hopping like a sparrow'. Lady Cunard was extraordinarily well-read, with a quick wit and a sharp tongue, her parties were small and intimate and she mixed her guests in a way that others might have thought socially hazardous. She was not bothered, for instance, with balancing the numbers of men and women—her parties, she said, were 'for conversation, not for mating'. 'She was usually slightly late for them,' says her biographer, Daphne Fielding, 'and would arrive, poking her head round the door to peer with an expression of pleased surprise at the assembled guests.' She gave them nicknames and introduced them to one another in an unorthodox way—'This is Lord Berners, a saucy fellow' or 'Here's little Poppy. Everyone's crazy about little Poppy.' Osbert Sitwell said, 'She can goad the conversation as if it were a bull and she a matador and compel it to show a fiery temper'.

Her clothes were fashionable. Before she dressed for dinner in the evening her maid would brush silver powder through her hair to make it glitter. But her pride was her white skin, and her greatest extravagance was beauty treatments and creams for her face. Whenever possible—sometimes every day—she would visit the exclusive London beautician Countess Csaky.

Two men figured in her life. The writer George Moore loved her from the moment they met at a luncheon party when she had switched the place cards to put herself next to him. But her life's passion was Sir Thomas Beecham. Because of him she became a serious patron of the opera, bullying her unmusical friends into subscribing for boxes at Covent Garden. The affair lasted for years before he broke her heart by marrying someone else. A chance remark at a party gave her the news; Emerald Cunard confided in her hostess that she wanted only to die.

When the Prince of Wales fell in love with Wallis Simpson, Lady Cunard fostered and encouraged the Royal romance— she rather saw herself in the role of the future Queen's favourite. But King Edward abdicated and, as a popular jingle went at the time, 'the Ladies Colefax and Cunard/Took it very very hard'.

As far as the new King and Queen went, Lady Cunard had rather burnt her boats. Shortly after the Coronation The Queen was supposed to have said, 'I am afraid even now we shall never be included in Lady Cunard's set. You see she has so often said that Bertie and I are not fashionable.'

3 A Whirl Through Wonderland

If you were to read all the newspaper gossip columns from 1930 until the end of the fifties you would find an extraordinary amount of space devoted to the doings of the debutante; what she wore, how many guests attended her parties, who were her admirers, how much Mummy and Daddy had spent on launching her. It seems odd that anyone outside her immediate social circle should have been remotely interested in all this; after all, she was nothing more than an upper-crust girl whose emergence was marked in England by a presentation at Court, and by a set of formal social engagements from which most readers of the newspapers would have been unquestionably excluded.

The debs themselves obviously revelled in their publicity, but they couldn't understand it any better than I can. Brenda Frazier, whose fame in America in 1938 gave her the status of a national monument, said at the time, 'I am not a celebrity. I don't deserve all this. I haven't done anything spectacular. I haven't done anything at all. I am just a debutante.' And Margaret Whigham, whose coming out in London had attracted the same degree of publicity in 1930, commented, 'I would like to be able to say that my generation had done something serious and useful at this time, but I am afraid that we were butterflies without a serious thought in our heads.'

Actually there *was* a serious motive behind all the brouhaha of a debutante's coming out, and that was to hook a good husband. 'Unless I married well,' said Brenda Frazier, 'the whole thing would have been in vain.' To that end, mothers would pawn their jewellery and fathers would take out a second mortgage on the family home. Bringing out a daughter was no cheap affair. In the fifties it was estimated that by the time you had hired a London house with a smart address for the season, paid for a coming-out ball, and for the huge wardrobe of clothes needed for all these social functions at which your daughter would meet the same set of people over and over and over again, you could be poorer by as much as £8,000.

The cheapest (free in fact) but by far the most important part for an English deb was the Presentation at Court. Your social status could not really be questioned after you had curtseyed to The King or Queen. 'From that august interview', Thackeray wrote in *Vanity Fair*, 'they come out stamped as honest women. The Lord Chamberlain gives them a certificate of virtue.' Or as the gossip columnist of the *Daily Express* put it: 'Without that presentation a girl could scarcely be offered on the marriage market as first class.'

Madame Vacani corrects the posture of a debutante in the fifties.

Left: Margaret Whigham in 1930, the year of her debut. She is considered to have been the prettiest and the most popular of all the British debutantes.

Only a woman who had herself been presented could present a new deb at Court. This simple rule kept the whole thing as untainted by outsiders as possible, though at one time after the Second World War a few women illicitly began charging fees to present girls who had no friends or relations qualified to do so. Before the Second World War presentations were made in the evening and the young debs wore white court dresses— 'The train must not exceed two yards in length' was the rule— and three white feathers mounted as a Prince of Wales plume in their hair. After the War the presentations took place in the afternoon at more informal Garden Parties. Although I was never a proper deb—I didn't 'do the season' as it was called—I was presented along with several hundred other girls at one of these parties in 1957. I wore a navy blue dress and a hat of pink flowers and naked terror has wiped most of the event from my mind, though I do recall feeling rather smug as our car was waved through the gates of Buckingham Palace, and I can remember my knees cracking like pistol shots in the Throne room as I lowered myself into a curtsey in front of first The Queen and then Prince Philip.

Right: Brenda Frazier, in 1938, the year she became so famous in America that a special word had to be coined to describe her status—celebutante.

Debs' mothers were notorious and terrifying snobs. With their daughter's whole future at stake they simply could not afford to put a foot wrong socially. Certain rituals grew up over the years and became The Done Thing. It was The Done Thing for instance to have your daughter's portrait taken by a leading society photographer, and this in turn could lead to the most sought-after type of publicity, for the photographers sent pictures to the society magazines, the *Tatler, Bystander, Country Life, Weekly Sketch*, who published the ones they liked or considered important.

Lenare was a favourite photographer until his studio closed in 1976. He photographed the debs on their coming out, and then again when they became engaged. He probably did their wedding pictures and photographed their first babies, and then did portraits of these babies when they in turn grew up to be debutantes. Lenare was, in fact, Mr Leonard Green who opened a studio in 1924, off Hanover Square. He was joined in 1931 by John Cawthorne, who carried on the tradition of flattering soft-focus pictures which were all carefully retouched so that even the plainest girl came out looking something special. No colour photography was ever done here—it was thought too crude, and besides, it might be unflattering. Instead a colourist would delicately paint in by hand the faintest blush in the cheeks, the rose-red lips and blue eyes. No one really knows why Lenare's became *the* studio, but everyone who was anyone seemed to pass through their discreet hands. 'Our heyday', says Mr Cawthorne, 'was in the grand court days. We would photograph the girls as soon as they came from the palace in their court dresses and feathers. The reception room would be crowded out with them and we would stay open specially until three in the morning until the last girl was done. We kept brandy on hand to revive the girls that drooped.' A Lenare coming-out portrait is immediately identifiable: there is the usual mistiness about it, a sort of halo of light round the girl's head, perhaps some flowers to give a fresh look, and the girl always has the train of her court dress over her arm.

It was The Done Thing to send your daughter to Madame Vacani for her curtseying lessons. Madame Vacani was a very grand dancing teacher, who opened her studio before the First World War and taught generations of Royal children to polka and waltz—including the Queen, Prince Charles and Princess Anne. She specialized in showing debutantes how to cope with their presentation curtseys. In the Court days, before the Second World War, she always kept curtains in her studio to pin on as trains and Prince of Wales feathers for the hair, so that the girls could practise in the same sort of outfit as they would be wearing on the great day itself. Madame Vacani retired, at least from strenuous teaching, at the end of the War in 1945 but her niece Betty carries on the studio to this day.

It was The Done Thing in the thirties to book Ambrose and his orchestra to play at your daughter's coming-out dance, and in the fifties you tried for Tommy Kinsman's band. But long before these plans were laid your daughter had to attend a finishing school. Switzerland, Munich, Paris and Florence were the snob places. Now, on finishing schools I am, as it were, the horse's mouth. Rather more by accident than design I was sent to finish at what, in the fifties, was considered to be the smartest school of all: Mademoiselle Anita's in Paris.

Mademoiselle Anita was an elderly lady of mysterious background—I never even knew her surname. She stood ramrod straight with her hair in a bun and governed her unruly bunch of adolescent girls with inflexible authority. Her establishment was the annexe to a convent in the smart *seizième* district of Paris and she took a few boarders and a host of day girls. Blue-blooded princesses, countesses and baronesses mingled with the daughters of South American millionaires and Asian political leaders. My schoolfriends were called Hohenlohe, Metternich, von Bismark, and Lowenstein. When one of them left to marry a Hapsburg prince, she sent back wedding snaps which showed her leaving the church in a golden coach drawn by six white horses, her bridegroom in a cloth-of-gold cape and a mink hat.

Henrietta Tiarks, best-known of the post-War debs, photographed in 1957, the year she came out.

42

I can't remember learning anything more exotic than history of art, geography, history, and of course French, unless you count Mademoiselle Anita's weekly talks to her boarders called *Savoir Vivre*. At these we heard about the hundreds of girls in Paris who disappear into White Slavery every year, and were warned that if you gave a man your little finger he would seize your whole body.

Every afternoon a crocodile of girls, always in gloves and with horsey headscarves knotted on the chin, was led off by a long-suffering elderly chaperone to the Louvre, or to the Père Lachaise cemetery, or to some other museum where we larked about behind her back. Bridge and cookery were optional extras my parents could not afford so I cannot vouch for how well-finished those pupils emerged. I once got a wedding invitation from some family friends but was not allowed to go. Mademoiselle inspected the invitation and declared it rather common. If a boy wanted to take one of us out, he had to be interviewed by Mademoiselle first. (I didn't actually know any boys so that didn't bother me.) The day girls were mostly English and next year's batch of debs. One of them, Henrietta Tiarks, became Deb of the Year. Another girl, Tessa Kennedy, was one of the first of what the papers called 'run-away heiresses'—she eloped to marry Dominic Elwes.

The vintage years for debutantes were between 1930 and 1957, for it was during this time that the newspapers gave the girls star treatment. By 1930 the most written-about, talked-about and frequently photographed deb was know as the Deb of the Year, and this was a title yearned after by the upper-class seventeen-year-olds. Margaret Whigham who came out in 1930 was undoubtedly the most famous—so famous in fact, that it was rumoured that her father had hired a press agent, a piece of gossip the Whigham family hotly denied.

Miss Whigham's debut was made alongside two other beauties, Rose Bingham and Lady Bridget Poulett, but she outshone both of them. Miss Whigham was described as 'quite the smartest *jeune fille* London had seen for a long time', and she later said that her coming-out year was 'a whirl through wonderland'. Miss Whigham's father was a successful business-man and she had been brought up in New York, but at the time of her debut in society her parents were living at Ascot, though of course they rented a smart house in London to see their daughter through her season. She was undoubtedly a beautiful girl, with grey eyes, Cupid's bow lips and a strong determined face. By the time she married the American Charles Sweeny in 1933 she had become such a public figure that enormous crowds gathered outside the Brompton Oratory and the cars caused a memorable traffic jam. As she walked down the aisle in a Norman Hartnell dress of ivory satin, which seamstresses had spent six weeks embroidering with seed pearls, two hundred unruly gate-crashers stood on the pews and clung to the pillars to get a better view. A *Sunday Graphic* reporter wrote: 'I discovered in the crowds that fought to see her married, scores of

Rose Bingham came out in 1930 and featured in the society columns of the newspapers almost as often as Margaret Whigham. She was a close rival for the title Deb of the Year. She married the Earl of Warwick – who had previously been engaged to Miss Whigham.

Primrose Salt was Deb of the Year in 1933. She was invited to do modelling work, but her dislike of being photographed soon ended that career. One newspaper, unable to book Miss Salt herself, superimposed her face on their fashion pictures. To this day she does not understand what sparked off the adulation that attended her debut.

young women who had obviously modelled their appearance on hers. They had long earrings, full, rich, Cupid bow lips and tiny hats aslant as "the Whigham" wears them. I watched them scan her avidly to get "confirmation" for few had actually seen her except in photographs. I think this imitation is certainly the highest form of flattery, and usually reserved for film stars.'

As Mrs Charles Sweeny she remained in the limelight. She and her husband were it seems 'the best-known couple outside Royalty', and one version of Cole Porter's hit song of the period went:

> *You're the nimble tread of the feet of Fred Astaire,*
> *You're Mussolini,*
> *You're Mrs Sweeny,*
> *You're Camembert.*

Later on in life she was to experience, she wrote in her autobiography, times of 'near despair'. This happened in the sixties when she was the central figure in a sensational and scandalous divorce case brought against her by her second husband, the Duke of Argyll.

Across the Atlantic there was no King or Queen to curtsey to, but a debutante was launched with much the same lavish trimmings as her counterpart in London. Comparing the day in the life of an American deb in 1939 and an English one of 1955 reveals very little difference in their activities. Their day went something like this. Up at 11 or 11.30 a.m. and dress for a girls' lunch, usually with a fellow deb. Afternoon spent shopping, or attending a charity committee meeting, or writing thank-you letters. In the early evening a cocktail party, then dinner, and finally a dance. The only difference I can see is that American debs seemed to spend a good deal of time in night clubs and British debs were often forbidden them. 'Most mothers allow girls out with chaps alone only after their first season and then only to top-notch restaurants and clubs,' said a writer on etiquette.

Brenda Frazier was to America what Margaret Whigham was to Britain. A new word had to be coined to describe her fame—'celebutante'. Miss Frazier was selected as one of the eleven most glamorous people in the world in 1938, the year of her debut, and according to her citation, 'She made the American debutante the most attractive woman alive.'

Brenda Frazier talked in a high, shrill voice; she had a pale, photogenic face, shoulder-length dark hair, and favoured strapless evening dresses which soon became all the rage. She was seventeen in 1938 and was not the richest, nor the best bred, nor the most beautiful of that year's debutantes, but she was a nice combination of all three. No one quite knows why she became so extraordinarily famous, but whatever it was that nudged the ball, once it had started rolling nothing could stop it: 'I just can't keep her name out,' complained a gossip columnist. Miss Frazier had commissioned a press cuttings agency to keep track of any appearances she might make in the papers, but after her first six months in society they were snowed under by 5,000 different items. By the night of her own coming-out ball at the Ritz in New York her mother had decided to ban all photographers except one who would take pictures for the family album. Undaunted, the New York *Daily News* dressed six of its most attractive young men in tailcoats and supplied them with a room at the Ritz from which they could drift down casually to the ballroom (with their concealed cameras) and mingle with the thousand guests. The paper had the whole story in pictures before the last edition went to press. They raved over the ball, the food, the guests—and the expense which was said to be $60,000. It actually cost more like $16,000. Brenda Frazier appeared on the cover of *Life* magazine and was offered a film contract in Hollywood which she turned down. Fan mail for her poured in from all over the world. She was seen accompanied by Erroll Flynn, Douglas Fairbanks Junior and Howard Hughes, as well as a bevy of young men from well-to-do American families. Yet when she married quite quietly three years after her debut it ended in the divorce courts. Like Margaret Whigham, she had her years of near-despair and at the age of thirty-nine she tried to kill herself. She blamed her unhappiness on her childhood in which she had been a tug-of-love only child, constantly fought over by divorced and bitter parents, and on her astonishing debut—which she described as 'a horror'. Backed up by her mother, Brenda Frazier's daughter in her time refused to have an official debut.

The Second World War brought a temporary halt to the doings of the debs, but the whole rigmarole got back into gear again soon afterwards. It was now the turn of the young daughters of the thirties debutantes—most notably Frances Sweeny, Margaret Whigham's child, who was presented at court in 1955. But it was 1957, the last year of the Court presentations that produced the most exceptional crop of girls.

Frances Sweeny, Margaret Whigham's daughter made her own debut in 1955 and later married the Duke of Rutland. This Lenare portrait of her taken two years before her presentation is typical of the studio's style.

Suna Portman, in another typical Lenare portrait taken at the time of her presentation in 1957, and before she opted for a more unconventional life as a beatnik.

By that time there were two distinct types of debutante: the traditional deb who did all the right things and married well, and the wilder, less conventional deb whose escapades made just as many newspaper headlines. The most notorious of the latter was Suna Portman, Viscount Portman's niece and heiress to the Portman estates. In spite of being known as 'The Girl Who Had Everything', Miss Portman chose to lead a bohemian life; she worked as an art student, a painter and a part-time waitress. In those days people who dressed as she did were known as beatniks, and among her contemporaries in Chelsea she was thought of as a fashion leader—though inevitably their elders frowned disapprovingly on their untidy clothes and the disreputable lives they were supposed to lead. Miss Portman had long, blonde hair which she left hanging loose, and she habitually wore a baggy, black sweater, tight blue jeans and day–glo red socks. Her shoes were said to be so dirty that no one could tell what colour they were.

Of the quieter, more ladylike girls Henrietta Tiarks was by far the most celebrated. She was the sweet-looking, pug-faced daughter of a London banker, and the fashion ideal of those who didn't care to copy Ms Portman's raffish style. Her bouffant hair was always immaculately coiffed, she dressed prettily but not startlingly, and she wore discreet yet modern make-up.

In 1957 the Queen stopped the presentation parties forever, and it fell to Miss Tiarks to become the very last Deb of the Year; as such she could be said to have become the Deb of the Decade. Her season had the right result, and she married the Marquis of Tavistock.

With the end of Court presentations for debutantes the season could never be quite the same. As the *Daily Express* William Hickey column said (and it is appropriate to give the last word on this subject to a gossip columnist): 'There will still be a debutante world, but something of the glamour and the exclusiveness will have disappeared forever. Goodbye, Darlings.'

47

4 For They Have the Faces of Angels

Britain may not breed the kind of long-legged, thoroughbred women who grace the annual Best-Dressed lists, but ever since St Gregory noticed the blonde Anglo-Saxon children in the slave market in Rome and remarked that they looked like angels, we have been a nation renowned for a particular type of cool blonde beauty.

By an odd coincidence, the two women who have done more to enhance this reputation than anyone else had the same name, were born within four years of each other and lived on to great old age without losing a bit of their charm and fascination. Gladys Cooper and Diana Cooper were not related to each other, but they shared the same exquisite English looks of flaxen hair, blue eyes and fair skin.

A friend of mine once told me that his mother used to pray on her knees every night in front of a picture of Gladys Cooper. 'Oh God make me look like her', she would murmur again and again. My own mother was taken to see Gladys Cooper acting in *The Last of Mrs Cheyney* and wearing beautiful gowns Molyneux had designed for her role. My grandmother considered the play a little risqué for her teenage daughter and told her quite firmly that she was not to listen at all to the words said on stage, just to look at the clothes Miss Cooper wore. To those who now only remember her as a respected Dame of the theatre, it must seem strange that at one time, half Britain wanted to look like this woman. Fan letters, simply addressed 'Gladys Cooper, England', arrived without difficulty.

In her time, Gladys Cooper played as many parts off the stage as on. She first came before the public as an Edwardian picture postcard beauty, coyly posing as a shepherdess or shyly peeping out of a window framed with roses. Her son-in-law, Robert Morley, says that one of his favourites is rather daring. It shows Miss Cooper with her long hair in plaits and wearing a peignoir over a wrap over a nightdress, on the point of opening a bedroom door. Later in her life her fans used to send these cards back to her, and she would be most suspicious of them. 'I don't think that is me at all,' she would tell her family, 'I'm sure there was another woman who used to pose as me at times.'

Her early years in the theatre were spent as a Gaiety chorus girl, an understudy, and playing small parts in musical comedy. She was married to Herbert Buckmaster, founder of Buck's, one of the most famous of the London gentlemen's clubs, and inventor of the drink Buck's Fizz, a mixture of champagne and fresh orange juice. Her first cracking success came in 1922, in

Gladys Cooper at the height of her beauty and influence, wearing one of the superbly elegant dresses that designer Molyneux created specially for her stage roles.

49

The Second Mrs Tanqueray. She was already thirty-four years old: elegance and maturity were admired more in those days. *The Times* described the evening as a great one for the ex-Gaiety Girl who had proved it was possible to be the most beautiful woman in the theatre and to act as well. It was during this middle period of her life that her beauty was most influential— 'She's the loveliest thing I've ever seen in my life,' said Somerset Maugham who wrote several of the hit plays she appeared in. (One of them, *The Sacred Flame*, was condemned by the Bishop of London as being the most immoral play in town.) It was at this time, during the second half of the twenties, that women craved to look like her; and indeed, glancing at old family pictures, they seemed to succeed quite well: her short, waved hair worn with a side-parting seems to crown every head.

Miss Cooper was one of the first great beauties to capitalize on her looks. In 1924 she opened a beauty shop selling 'Gladys Cooper's Beauty Preparations'. 'I am always having letters from people who ask my advice about skin and complexion treatment, and as I do happen to know something about the subject it occurred to me that I might turn my knowledge to good account. I do not propose to give the public things I haven't tried on myself. Everything has been carefully tested . . .' The venture went successfully at first, but ended in the courts, where after much bickering and acrimony between Miss Cooper and her partner, the company's debts were paid and it was wound up.

By 1938 Gladys Cooper was married to her third husband, actor Philip Merivale, and in that year was invited to film *Rebecca* in Hollywood. She stayed on through the War, and from being totally unknown to American filmgoers, she came to receive more fan letters than she had ever had. In 1948 she reappeared on the English stage and from then until her death in 1971 she was the grandest old lady of the British theatre.

Her professionalism was as famous as her beauty and there is a touching story to illustrate it. On her eightieth birthday, Miss Cooper was playing at the St Martin's Theatre in London. Unknown to her, the management had bought back every seat in the house that night and filled them with Miss Cooper's family and friends. At a point in the play at which her stage grandson should have appeared, Robert Morley, who was not in the cast at all, walked on stage carrying a tray clinking with glasses of champagne. Miss Cooper was appalled, and thinking this must be some naughty prank, she told him in angry whispers to go away, get off. Only when she was completely convinced that the audience was entirely of invited guests was she prepared to stop acting and enjoy her birthday surprise.

When I knocked at the door of Lady Diana Cooper's house in Little Venice, London, there was a long wait before a firm voice called out: 'I am going to open the door but you are *not* to look at me. I am simply awful today.' Of course, I not only looked, I stared. It is not every morning one meets a living legend and one must make the best of such encounters.

The astonishingly beautiful Lady Diana Cooper photographed in 1925. She made her name as an actress in *The Miracle* in the role of a statue that comes to life.

That was in the Spring of 1976. Lady Diana was eighty-four years old and she entertained me in her bedroom wearing a luxurious lace-trimmed nightdress and bedjacket and lying between silk sheets. Her face (which has been compared to a Botticelli angel's) was powdered white, carefully made up and still lovely. No wonder when Cecil Beaton met her in Venice in her heyday in 1926, he wrote, 'Surely she must be the most beautiful Englishwoman alive today. I stared in awe. Her face was a perfect oval, her skin white marble. Her lips were japonica red, her hair flaxen, her eyes blue love-in-the-mist.'

Diana Cooper seems to have borne the burden of great beauty with charm and intelligence. There is a nice moment in her memoirs, where she tells of looking in the mirror one morning and seeing her face haggard with tiredness—'That's over,' she says in a no-nonsense way, 'now it's nap on personality.' Throughout her life, instead of resenting this privileged and gifted woman, both men and women alike have been bewitched by her.

51

Lady Diana was a daughter of the Duke of Rutland but instead of leading the kind of social life you would expect from a high-born beauty, culminating of course, in a 'good' marriage, she chose to become an actress. In the very early twenties she made two films, both costume dramas. In one she played Elizabeth I, and the critics said that though Lady Diana was far too good-looking for the part of the Virgin Queen, 'she deserves her place as a film star because of her ability as an actress, not merely because she is a celebrity of society.'

Her mother was an artistic lady who belonged to a fashionable intellectual group called 'The Souls' and wore trailing robes and a Greek hairstyle. As a child Diana Manners was dressed in the most unconventional clothes. She became used to being the centre of attraction. When other little girls wore white muslin, Lady Diana was dressed in black velvet; at Ascot races, instead of a simple straw, she wore a black hat trimmed with ears of gold and silver wheat; and when Lady Diana was asked to appear at a fancy dress pageant as one of a group of swans, her mother made sure she was the only black one. As if this wasn't enough, 'Odd things always seemed to be happening to me. I'd fall through a skylight or something . . . I was always in the papers. That is what gave me the part in *The Miracle*—the best thing in my life.'

The Miracle was a highly symbolic play—without any words —in which a statue of the Madonna comes to life in a cathedral and descends from its plinth. Max Reinhardt chose Diana Cooper to play the Virgin for an American tour with half an eye on the publicity it would give the play to have a real English Duke's daughter in it. Though a few frowned on her accepting the part for just that reason, *The Miracle* made Diana Cooper into an international celebrity.

In the meantime Lady Diana had defied her family to marry Duff Cooper, a foreign office clerk whom her family considered far beneath her. (Her mother had to be sedated at the news of her engagement.) But the marriage was vindicated, Duff Cooper became First Lord of the Admiralty and, immediately after the Second World War, British Ambassador to Paris.

Surprisingly, Lady Diana says she never cared much for clothes. As a young girl she made her own: 'We were never taught to cook, but we could all sew. I could cut out a shirt before lunch.' Later she dressed at Madame Ospovat, a Russian designer in London—'She dressed me free. We never spent anything on clothes then. It was thought awful to do so.'

Perhaps it was her mother's influence, but Diana Cooper has always dressed rather unconventionally, more in the relaxed way that girls do now than they did then. During the War her delight was tending to the farm animals she had imported to her home in Bognor. Cecil Beaton watched her milking the cow, Princess, and commented that in her stained dungarees of blue canvas, headscarf and straw hat she looked quite as beautiful as she ever did in *The Miracle*. The one time she did buy what she called 'like other people's dresses' and 'humourless hats' was before she left for the Embassy in Paris. 'I must try not to swell the list of mad English Ambassadresses,' she wrote.

Hats have always been her trademark. 'I like to feel covered,' she says. 'My hats are glued on.' The more eccentric the hat the better. Even in her eighties she still wears the Royal Yacht Squadron peaked cap that she had when Duff Cooper became First Sea Lord. She has giant picture hats, a hat made of coconut fibre, coolie hats, and an old frilled cotton bonnet which ties under the chin. During the War when women wore head-scarves, Lady Diana managed to tie hers so that it never looked quite like anyone else's.

In her old age she has rather shunned publicity, but a rare newspaper picture of her at the funeral of a friend in the early seventies was as reassuring as the Ravens at the Tower of London. There stood the aged beauty in a sad group of mourn-ers, but upright and slender in a newly fashionable black maxi-coat, boots, and a dramatic black hat with a veil.

They called her marriage to Duff Cooper 'the love affair of the century', but she was also unwittingly involved in what must be the unrequited love affair of the age—the strange passion for Lady Diana that possessed the heart of the Count of Lazarraga. This gentleman had only seen her once, in the street, but he wrote to her for twenty-five years without ever receiving a reply, and when he died he left Lady Diana £25,000.

Left and *Below:* Lady Diana has always had a passion for hats. Her collection includes antique cotton bonnets, frivolous net affairs, face-shading straws, and the famous peaked cap of the Royal Yacht Squadron, which she acquired when her husband was First Lord of the Admiralty, and which, in her eighties, she still jauntily wears.

5 The Good, the Bad and the Ugly

My uncle used to advise the female members of his family that if they couldn't be the best-dressed women in a room they should at least make an effort to be the worst-dressed: then they certainly wouldn't pass unnoticed altogether. His thinking was not entirely original for there have always been women who have decided to dress outrageously, flamboyantly, even idiotically. Actresses have done it for publicity, ugly women have done it to draw attention away from their faces, fashionable women

Left: Paloma Picasso belongs to an undeniably stylish family. A fashion editor described her once as 'striking in an ugly sort of way' and she has become one of those In people on the chic fringes of the international fashion world: designing jewellery, dressing at Saint Laurent, making frequent appearances in glossy magazines and taking part in the occasional underground movie.
Right: The Marquesa Casati, queen of the eccentrics. She had a Tunisian 'slave' boy, kept a monkey in her salon and snakes slithered freely around the stone floor of her house.

have done it to maintain their positions as innovators and leaders, and rebels have done it to prove how little they care for conventional opinion. To be a success, dressing eccentrically or differently requires a steady nerve and a good deal of personality and style—and those are the characteristics the women in this chapter have in common.

Edna Woolman Chase of American *Vogue* once wrote: 'Fashion can be bought, style one must possess. Some women have it. Some haven't.' One has only to look around to see what she meant. Even at school where we were all dressed identically in hideous striped blazers and green skirts, there were some girls who looked positively distinguished, and some, like me, who were just part of the crowd, shuffling around with egg stains on their ties and hems hanging down at the back.

In the old days it was hard to be daring unless you had the hallmarks of good breeding and/or a great deal of money to back you up. No one thought Princess de Faucigny Lucinge vulgar because she wore jewels on her bathing suit—quite the opposite, it was considered *frightfully* witty. On the other hand, when the Dolly Sisters wore diamonds in Cannes, it was frowned on as common. And it was only *after* her marriage to a Roman aristocrat that the notorious Marquesa Casati let rip and gained her reputation as queen of the eccentrics. Before that, as the plain daughter of a Milan industrialist, she had been described as mousey and unremarkable.

Her transformation was breathtaking. Marquesa Casati dyed her hair bright red, ringed her eyes with black kohl, wore false eyelashes as long as feathers, painted her face a deathly white and her lips blood red. She took to wearing platform-soled shoes and hats like wastepaper baskets turned upside down, and chose the most daring creations that such designers as Léon Bakst could invent. She once planned to attend a fancy-dress ball dressed as Saint Sebastian in armour pierced with arrows— these were to light up when she made her entrance—and she arrived in advance of the other guests with an electrician in tow. But when the costume was plugged in the Marquesa lit up instead of the arrows. She did not recover in time for the party. Cecil Beaton tells how she once arrived to visit him in the English countryside in the middle of winter when snow was all around, wearing an enormous cowboy hat, white flannel trousers and gold sandals.

Overpowering and witch-like though she was, the Marquesa Casati conquered the heart of the poet and lover Gabriel d'Annunzio, and in 1919 she left her husband to become his mistress. By the thirties she had squandered several fortunes and came to live alone in London in a small, dirty flat in Piccadilly. Her clothes grew shabbier and full of holes and she only managed to survive with the help of friends like Augustus John, who had known her (and painted her) in better days. But her friends said the Marquesa never lost her spirit. Augustus John once remarked to Cecil Beaton that she deserved to be stuffed and put in a glass case.

Some of the more eccentrically-dressed women in the twenties were Paula Gellibrand (*top*) who once went to the Savoy in a hat covered with wisteria blossom, and was married in a garment that looked like a nun's habit; Lady Abdy (*right*) who was six foot tall but dressed to accentuate her height rather than disguise it, and Baba de Faucigny Lucinge (*far right*) who was considered to be rather plain but the very essence of chic.

Among the rich and well-dressed society women based in Paris in the twenties and thirties, there were a few who enjoyed pushing fashion to its limits. They specialized in a kind of uncompromising, hard-edged smartness which certainly needed style to carry off successfully. They revelled in being the ones less daring women talked about, and copied if they had the nerve. Baba de Faucigny Lucinge was the best known. Rude and snobbish though she was, whatever she wore made news. 'She looked like a monkey,' I was told by a woman who knew her well, 'she had an ugly little face, but my God she really had chic if anybody had.' Someone who liked her less said, 'She was a selfish little woman and her teeth were too big for her mouth'.

Princess Faucigny Lucinge played up to her odd looks by dressing in severe clothes, usually by Lucien Lelong, adopting strange hairstyles, and concentrating on dramatic hats (which were designed *on* her head by Madame Suzy). Bettina Ballard, American *Vogue's* correspondent in Paris, wrote, 'When she ran her middle part down the back of her head and rolled her hair in shells over her ears, or when she painted only the very tips of her nails red, she was slavishly copied.'

She had a most peculiar upbringing in London. Her mother, Baroness d'Erlanger, sent her for walks not with a nanny, but with a Mameluke servant dressed in a turban and coloured robes. Baba was friendly with a young woman named Paula Gellibrand, and the Baroness like the girls to be seen together. She thought Paula Gellibrand's striking, blonde beauty set off her own daughter's dark looks to perfection, and encouraged the girl to dress as curiously as her daughter: when Paula Gellibrand married the Marquis de Casa Maury she went to her wedding dressed like a nun. Lady Diana Cooper remembers Baba d'Erlanger as 'always so amusingly dressed—to me she looked like a ·Berber Arab youth—someone from another world. She had the same effect on me as Iya Abdy.'

Iya Abdy was startling to look at because she was over six feet tall and yet, apart from wearing low-heeled shoes, made no concessions to her height. Cecil Beaton recollects her in a voluminous cape of sable that flowed to the ground, and with a penchant for enormous felt hats.

She was the daughter of a famous Russian actor and was one of the many emigrés who found their way to Paris after the Russian Revolution. Toto Koopman still thinks of her as one of the most remarkable-looking women of the time. 'She was quite extraordinary, like a giant blonde Garbo. She wore very simple clothes but always chose odd hats. She was a tremendous friend of Chanel who dressed her for nothing because she looked so good and knew all the right people.' One wonders how the couturiers made any money when so many of their clients acted as unofficial mannequins and were clothed free.

I can think of only one modern woman who dresses in the hard, sure, chic way of these ultra-smart women of the twenties and thirties. That is Bianca Jagger, the Nicaraguan beauty who in 1971 married the British pop idol in St Tropez wearing a

Bianca Jagger, fanatically and fastidiously chic.

see-through shirt. Mrs Jagger could be the reincarnation of someone like Baba de Faucigny Lucinge, except that her face is prettier. She is a notoriously difficult woman, and recently her tantrums, walkouts and script changes allegedly caused a film company to scrap a movie at a cost of £400,000. The director complained that Valentino, the Italian designer in charge of Mrs Jagger's film wardrobe, 'gets more time with the leading lady than I do.'

Bianca Jagger has a reputation for being compulsively un-punctual. She can be two or three hours late for a lunch date, two or three *days* late for appointments that involve longer journeys. Her excuse is simply the time it takes her to get ready, for she is fanatically chic and goes to great pains to achieve the look she is after—when she favoured mannish, tailored jackets and trousers, for instance, she was always seen carrying an antique inlaid walking cane. The English designer Ossie Clark used to be her favourite, but after disagreements with him she turned to Yves Saint Laurent. When she rowed with him she went to Valentino. Luckily her break with him coincided with the Jaggers' move to the United States where, last heard of, Mrs Jagger was shopping at Halston, the New York designer.

On the Left Bank of the Seine in Paris, far from the elegant drawing rooms and couture-clad ladies of the fashionable world, there has always existed another, more relaxed society com-posed of writers, actors, artists, dancers, and musicians, for whom creativity counts more than class. Nancy Cunard, poet and writer, belonged to it, though by virtue of her birth and

Nancy Cunard, daughter of the famous hostess Emerald Cunard, turned her back on her mother's way of life to live in Paris among writers and poets. Her startling make-up and unconventional way of dressing were greatly admired, and among the fashions she launched was a craze for leopardskin.

Zizi Jeanmaire in 1972, aged 47 and still wearing the cropped *gamine* hairstyle she had made famous almost thirty years before.

breeding she could have been just as comfortably part of the smart set on the Right Bank. She was the daughter of Lady Emerald Cunard, the famous hostess, but as unlike her mother as a cat is to a canary. Her childhood in England had been strict and miserable and from an early age Nancy Cunard set her face against her mother's kind of life. She infinitely preferred talking to her friends in cafés, Bloomsbury garrets, Limehouse pubs, even cab shelters, to meeting the rich and famous in society salons. In 1922, the year after her first volume of poetry was published, Nancy Cunard settled in Paris, where her striking looks and unconventional dress were much admired among her Left Bank contemporaries. She liked leopardskin; she dyed her hair golden and had it cut short to curve in two points over her cheeks; she ringed her startling blue eyes with kohl; and she crowded her arms with ivory and ebony bracelets from Africa which clacked together like billiard balls when she moved.

Nancy Cunard was a passionate champion of underdog causes, and in particular she campaigned for justice and equality for black people. Of all her many unorthodox adventures, nothing shocked society more than her affair with Henry Crowther, a negro pianist. It was this that led to her lifelong feud with her mother. Lady Cunard had the couple followed when they came to London, they were asked to leave their lodgings, and were persecuted by anonymous letters and telephone calls. The trip was misery and in revenge Nancy published a pamphlet denouncing her mother in bitter language. Emerald only said, 'One can always forgive someone who is ill.'

Nervous and unstable, Nancy was too often ill. She barely ate, smoked heavily and her neurotic scenes and sudden rages were notorious. She wandered around the world all her life— to North Africa, South America, to Harlem in New York with Henry Crowther, and to Spain where she was a Civil War correspondent for the *Manchester Guardian*. On a trip to London in 1960 she was arrested in the Kings Road for drunk and disorderly behaviour. She kicked a policeman, and took off her shoes in court and threw them at the magistrate. She was certified insane and sent for treatment, but she recovered and left the mental institution, a sad old woman, short of money and with failing health. 'One's body should not be felt,' she had once said, but hers was letting her down. In March 1965, she was found dying in a street in Paris. Only a handful of people attended the funeral: 'A sad lonely farewell to a toast of the twenties,' said a newspaper report of the burial.

When I was at school in the fifties, we all wanted to look like another Left Bank character—Zizi Jeanmaire. She and her husband Roland Petit were ballet dancers. They belonged in an artistic and creative *milieu* in Paris, and her face would probably never have been known to middle-class English girls like us if she had not appeared with Danny Kaye in the musical *Hans Christian Andersen*. That film made her kind of look popular. She was the original *gamine*—the petite boyish-girl with a close-cropped cap of black hair, huge eyes and a wide mouth. So pert and sharp—very different to our other insipid heroines—she seemed to sum up everything French. Richard Buckle, the ballet critic, once called her 'the most attractive woman in the world'.

Zizi Jeanmaire's unique style was created by accident nearly thirty years ago when she was in her twenties. She was to dance in her husband's production of *Carmen* and he wanted her hair very, very short. 'When I hesitated he just took some scissors and cut off all my long curly hair. I was horrified—nobody had such short hair in those days—but in a way I seemed to find my personality then.'

I met her when she was forty-seven and dazzling audiences every night in a lavish revue at the Casino de Paris. Backstage, wearing a glittering sequin leotard, her beautiful legs in sheer black stockings, she was oiling and smoothing down the same glossy black hair, and her face was as animated and attractive as I remembered it from long ago. Only a Frenchwoman, I thought, would dare to make absolutely no concessions to her age and get away with it.

A touch of studied eccentricity has never done an actress any harm, and, fully aware of this, no one worked harder at her image than the extrovert revue artist Andrée Spinelly, known simply as Spi to her many fans up to and during the twenties and thirties. Like Zizi Jeanmaire, Spi wore her hair short and slicked down with brilliantine, but there the resemblance ended, for Spi was less chic and far more theatrical. She had an exaggerated widow's peak touched up with pencil, a saucy

Andree Spinelly, photographed in 1926 when she came to England to take part in a Cochran revue. Her hallmarks were an exaggerated widow's peak, a long cigarette holder, and a beautiful body which she dressed eccentrically off the stage and daringly on it.

beauty spot on her cheek, and she smoked with an affectedly long cigarette holder. Her body was famous for its beauty. When Spi came to Britain to appear in a Cochran revue in 1926 she had it insured for £12,500: 'Sculptors have told me that it is a perfect replica of the Venus de Milo modernized,' she said, 'and I have received thousands of letters from American women asking me how I keep in such fine trim.' No one would have expected Spi's beauty secrets to be the least bit ordinary. They weren't. She claimed that she hung upside down from a trapeze every day before her bath, and that she always, but always, slept on the floor. This was curious, for it was known that Spi's bed was a luxurious affair surrounded by a gold fence with a gate in it that had to be unlocked before anyone could get in— but it was, Spi explained, simply to rest on during the day. Spinelly's house in Paris was as outrageous as anything in Hollywood; it was once described as a mixture of 'Hindu temple, Greek palace, Persian corner, and nightclub loggia'. In her hall, which was paved with gold mosaics, there was a pond full of exotic fish. (One day Spi discovered that her Great Dane, Faust, was lapping from it not only water but the live fish as well.)

Spinelly's stage clothes, designed to expose as much of the beautiful body as possible, were famous for their daring. She bought them all at the salon run by her famous actress friend Mistinguett. Once on stage her skimpy dress came off altogether—the audience adored that so much that a modified version of the incident had to be included in the show.

Spi behaved as boldly off the stage as on. A brief encounter with an Argentinian led to the birth of a baby boy. Brimming with curiosity and itching for scandal, reporters came to see her but Spinelly simply tossed her head and laughed: 'Three turns of a tango—oh, what a dangerous dance.'

In some families eccentricity and style run in the blood. Perhaps the most obvious examples are Maxime and Loulou de la Falaise, the daughter and granddaughter of Lady Rhoda Birley, who was herself a noted beauty, and no less unconventional than her offspring. (There is a story that she once cooked Lobster Thermidor and fed it to her roses. 'They love all sorts of shell things,' she said in explanation.)

In the forties, Maxime de la Falaise launched herself into the hectic post-War world of parties with zest and energy. She has worked as a fashion designer, a writer, even as an actress, playing a star part in Andy Warhol's *Dracula*. Now in her fifties, she is still travelling restlessly from America to Europe and back again, and still dressing her tall, slender frame with the uninhibited chic with which she has worn everything from Givenchy gowns 'done up with safety pins' to hippy clothes loaded with jewellery and scarves. Her daughter Loulou, she says, is her closest friend.

Tiny Loulou de la Falaise has become a well-known and most revered figure in the world of fashion. She first made her mark in London in the second half of the sixties when she was one of the first and most dazzling Flower Children, with wildly frizzed hair, dozens of layers of fabrics, plus beads, scarves, streamers—everything. Six years ago she unpredictably settled down to work with designer Yves Saint Laurent in Paris, and though her style changed (and she was even on the 1976 Best-Dressed list) it is no less extrovert. Ms de la Falaise handles clothes like no one else: she can switch from impeccably tailored jackets and skirts into jump suits or the wildest of gypsy outfits trailing all the trendiest bits and pieces. Her face is not particularly pretty, but it is interesting, rather small and hard. Not long ago I went to Saint Laurent's salon in Paris to do some pictures with David Bailey and for various reasons I had to take my small baby with me. Loulou eyed her coldly as she crawled among the gilt chairs and swung on the hems of the lavish dresses hanging on a rail, and I felt distinctively nervous. Having babies suddenly seemed like an awfully unchic thing to do.

Some of the most memorably-dressed women have found their style by simply turning their backs on convention and reversing the popular maxim to 'If you Can't Join 'Em—Beat 'Em'. At an early age the poet Edith Sitwell was aware that her long pale face and melancholy hooded eyes looked painfully ugly in conventional clothes: 'At my first ball I resembled a caricature of a Fairy Queen.'

Right: Tiger Morse, an American designer who came to fame in the early part of the sixties. She herself was far odder than any of the clothes she designed. *Below:* Loulou de la Falaise, daughter of the elegant Maxime, is Yves Saint Laurent's right hand woman and has an unerring sense of style.

Left: Julie Driscoll, the singer whose name was on everyone's lips towards the end of the sixties. Her hair was frizzed like wire wool, her eyes made up to look like stars, and her lips painted white. She had an obsession about health foods and even kept carrots in her handbag.
Right: Maxime de la Falaise photographed in 1950. She has always dressed with uninhibited chic, and passed her flair for clothes on to her daughter Loulou.

She felt herself to be a throwback to her Plantagenet ancestors and she decided to clothe herself accordingly. Dame Edith spent the whole of her life in what other people would describe as fancy dress, but it suited her extraordinarily medieval face to perfection. 'If I walked round in modern clothes,' she said, 'I would make people doubt the existence of God.' Since the wimples, turbans, Tudor hats and trailing robes she wore were not exactly the kind of things easily found in shops, she designed a good many of them herself and found the fabrics she liked in furnishing departments. It all began when she was eighteen in 1905 and was given her first money with which to buy clothes. 'I went to a sale,' she said, 'and bought a long black velvet dress with long sleeves. Everybody was quite horrified, for in those days young girls simply didn't wear black velvet. I realized at once the shock value of my long black velvet and I knew I was right to look different from the other girls because I *was* different. I think it is a mistake to dress like a mouse. Good taste is the worst vice ever invented.'

Diana Vreeland was not born a pretty woman either, but by shrewdly emphasizing all her worst points, she too achieved startling results. She was the powerful Editor-in-Chief of American *Vogue* before she retired, and was exactly what outsiders imagine fashion editors to be. With her theatrical gestures, exaggerations and *bon mots* ('Pink is the navy blue of India', for example), Diana Vreeland positively over-acted the part. A photographer once described her at work: 'She'd look at the clothes and then drift into a trance. "I see white," she'd moan, swaying about and stretching out for the word or item to perfect the picture.' A former colleague, Bettina Ballard, tells of the baffled look on a hairdresser's face when Mrs Vreeland explained in her deep, slow voice how she wanted a model's hair styled: 'Twist the hair up, twist it out . . . let it float into space—if you know what I mean—way, way out, all the way to Outer Mongolia.'

Mrs Vreeland's appearance, too, is most eccentric. The first time I saw her at the Paris Collections in the sixties my jaw dropped. She was middle-aged, but her hair was dyed a dense blue-black (it seems she always sleeps on a black pillow in order to leave no tell-tale trace) and it was scraped fiercely back from her face, for one of her unusual beliefs is that hairlines, together with hands, are the secret of elegance. She was dressed entirely in black, her nose was hooked like a Red Indian chief's, her cheeks highly rouged, and her mouth huge and mobile. She walked in the strangest way I've ever seen, balancing on tiny feet shod in odd little sandals, and with her pelvis pushed so far forward that the rest of her body slanted backwards. There was a visible air of authority about her—journalists in the salons were pushing and shoving to get to their seats, but in front of Mrs Vreeland the crowd parted like the Red Sea. I don't remember anyone else I saw that day, I can't even remember what the fashion designers showed; the only clear picture I have is of the unique, compelling figure of Diana Vreeland.

Diana Vreeland, whose wit, flair and extraordinary looks have made her one of the most arresting personalities in the fashion world. *Overleaf left*: Bettina Bergery in 1933, looked her best in Schiaparelli's eccentric designs. *Right*: Elsa Schiaparelli whose witty clothes were the talk of Paris in the thirties.

It is not surprising that in the ranks of the eccentrically dressed, one or two fashion designers take pride of place. It would be odd if among the women who have lived, breathed, and felt fashion more deeply than anyone else there weren't one or two who let it go to their heads.

Elsa Schiaparelli's unique and witty ideas made her clothes the most talked about and sought after in Paris in the thirties. 'A Schiaparelli customer did not have to worry as to whether she was beautiful or not, she was a type' said Bettina Ballard. 'She was noticed wherever she went, protected by an armour of amusing conversation-making smartness.'

Schiap, as she was known, was an Italian, born in Rome in 1896. Her marriage to a Pole took her to America. There it broke up, leaving Schiaparelli with a small daughter to support. (This daughter, Gogo, once described as a 'spoiled pet' who 'travelled with her own pink silk sheets', became the mother of Marisa Berenson, the model and film actress, and Berry Perkins, the photographer wife of Anthony Perkins.)

Schiaparelli moved to Paris and tried her hand at designing sweaters. In 1928 she produced her first really successful garment, a black, silky-knit jumper with an imitation white bow knitted in at the neck. Customers thought this extremely amusing and soon orders were piling up. The more outrageous Schiaparelli's ideas, the better everyone liked them. Each season Schiap produced a new theme—a Circus Collection for instance, or an Astrological Collection—and soon her theatrical shows were eagerly awaited. Her smart customers, like Mrs Reginald Fellowes and Millicent Rogers, took the best seats, while artists, writers, and musicians squashed together on the stairs: for all Paris was interested in her ideas. She collaborated with many of these people—Salvador Dali, for instance, who inspired her to make some surreal hats, including one like an upturned shoe and one like a frilled lamb cutlet. Schiap loved everything new and she was the first top designer to use synthetic fabrics and zip fasteners, the first to open a boutique (it was on the ground floor of the famous house she established in the Place Vendôme in 1934) and one of the first with the exaggerated wide shoulders that were fashionable at the end of the thirties and all through the War. But perhaps today we know her best as the inventor of the colour she christened Shocking Pink.

Schiap hired a young American girl as her assistant in the boutique, Bettina Jones, who later married a Frenchman and became Bettina Bergery. Uninhibited, slim and chic, she wore

Schiaparelli's daring clothes extremely well, and did much to make them popular. Bettina Bergery also had a name for being possessively jealous of her husband—she once stubbed a cigarette out on the back of a lady she suspected of flirting with him, and her pet monkey would attack any woman who seemed to be paying him too much attention.

American designer Tiger Morse (her real name was Joan) was a most bizarre lady, who came to fame briefly in the early part of the sixties before we had grown as accustomed to eccentrics as we are today. Unlike Schiaparelli, her own appearance was more curious than anything she produced in the way of clothes. She changed the colour of her hair eighteen times in as many months, and usually hid her eyes behind one of her eighty exotic pairs of sunglasses. Her face was made up with white rice powder, her lips were deathly pale and she often dressed from head to foot in tiger skins, though she would occasionally turn up in a glittering sari or a man's jacket and trousers. Her shop in New York was called A La Carte, and Tiger Morse encouraged her customers to use it as they did their own homes: 'They can come and go as they please,' she said, 'leave their dirty linen, iron their smalls, call in their hairdressers, eat, drink and do what they goddam like.'

When designer Zandra Rhodes emerged later in the sixties she made Tiger Morse look positively inhibited. Miss Rhodes was one of the many talents to emerge from London's Royal College of Art. She was known for her pretty fabric designs, and later, for astonishing floating fantasy clothes.

When I first knew her she was a mild-looking girl, not at all the type to turn heads, but as the sixties progressed Miss Rhodes became more and more eccentric to look at. If you had met her unexpectedly in 1969 you might have been forgiven for thinking that the Martians had landed. By then Miss Rhodes' hair was dyed in streaks of cerise, orange, blue and green, and she had given up her green false eyelashes in favour of painted-on rainbow stripes that stretched from eye to brow and down to her cheekbones. For good measure she also drew long red lashes beneath her eyes and finished the whole effect off with a bright pink dot on either cheek.

The sixties threw up more oddballs and eccentrics than any previous decade, a revolution was in progress and the public were hungry for new names and new faces. It did not take much to become famous in those days, a pop singer needed only the mildest of gimmicks to be picked out by the media and turned into a 'Personality'. For an instant a name would burn as brightly as a real star, only to disappear into obscurity the moment the next one came along. Who now remembers Helen Shapiro, as the 14-year-old schoolgirl who sang 'Please Don't Treat me Like a Child' in a throaty adult voice and instantly raced to the top of the charts in 1961? Her backcombed beehive hairdo swept the nation. Who remembers Julie Driscoll, the singer with the wild hair, white lips and eyes painted like stars who liked health foods and who lived with her

Right: Two unlikely fashion sources: Honor Blackman (*above*) appeared in *The Avengers* television series wearing sensational black leather outfits. Christine Keeler (*below*) was photographed for a *Daily Express* scoop story in 1963 wearing high-heeled black leather boots that were considered daringly kinky. *Below:* Helen Shapiro, the schoolgirl who sang in a throaty adult voice and whose beehive hairstyle swept the nation.

mother in a council flat in Lambeth? And who remembers Baby Jane Holzer, the 23-year-old American society girl who in 1964 became an In person, for no better reason than that she wore her hair backcombed more aggressively than anyone else? There was a time when you couldn't open a magazine without seeing her pretty face and tawny lion's mane. She modelled for *Vogue*, was featured in *Life* magazine, and appeared in underground films.

There was Sandie Shaw who hit the headlines because she sang in bare feet. And Cathy McGowan, known in 1965 as Queen of the Mods. (Who even remembers the Mods—those fashion-conscious kids who changed their style every week, knew each new dance the moment it arrived, and feuded with the Rockers who were only interested in motor bikes and black leather?) Cathy McGowan was compère of *Ready Steady Go*, a television pop programme that no teenager would have dreamt of missing. She got the job by answering an advertisement and at the height of her fame received a thousand fan letters a week for doing nothing more strenuous than talk and set the nation's teeth on edge by her continual use of the word 'Smashin''.

Two enduring fashions—for leather clothes and for boots—were set in the sixties by two unlikely women who dressed in a sexually uninhibited way, and had power of a kind that had not been openly boasted of before. From 1962 to 1964 Honor Blackman played the part of Cathy Gale in *The Avengers*, one of the most successful television series there has ever been. She dressed in black leather clothes of the type which up until then had only been seen in fetishist shops and in pornographic magazines. Cathy Gale did not only look like Miss Whiplash, she was a judo expert and threw men over her shoulder with unruffled efficiency, sending a masochistic thrill through her male viewers.

Christine Keeler's first appearance in the newspapers was in March 1963, shortly after she had failed to turn up as a witness at the trial in London of her West Indian lover. The *Daily Express* tracked the mysterious redhead to Spain where they photographed her looking arrogantly unrepentant and wearing high-heeled black leather boots, of the kind that are now fashionable but were still, in those days, thought of as kinky.

Miss Keeler was politely referred to as a 'free-lance model' in those early days, but we all knew better, and she came home from Spain to a Britain buzzing with rumours about what she was and who she knew. Endless press pictures showed her as a cool beauty with a knowing look and a teasing smile, and she sent pulses racing with excitement. Her name was linked with that of John Profumo, the Secretary of State for War, who made his historic denial to the House of Commons: 'There was no impropriety whatsoever in my acquaintanceship with Miss Keeler.' But too much was known, and before the story ended Mr Profumo had resigned in disgrace, Miss Keeler's protector, Stephen Ward, had committed suicide, and Christine Keeler herself was sent to prison for perjury.

6 The Spell of the Cinema

We take the cinema and television so much for granted nowadays that it is hard to imagine the first impact of the movies, the powerful spell they cast on film audiences, and the astonishing influence they gave to the early screen goddesses. It was the opening of the motion picture theatre in her own home town that gave the shop girl, the maid, the less privileged working woman her first glimpse of glamour and beauty. Part of the immense attraction was that up there on the screen, in intimate close-up, were real womens' faces with make-up and hairstyles that any ordinary person could imitate for herself. As *Vogue* said in 1937, 'The way you make up your lips, apply your rouge . . . ten to one it came from Hollywood and was devised either by or for some famous star.' By 1925 113,000,000 people were going to the films every week in America, and in Britain there were 3,500 movie palaces. No wonder every woman of that period seemed to have been born with the pencilled brows, prissy mouths and bobbed hair of their celluloid heroines.

Almost all the popular films in those days came from Hollywood and the beauty ideas were inspired by only a few famous stars. These women, in turn, were often in the hands of the man whose pioneering work in the art of make-up made him a household name—Max Factor. Max Factor was a Pole who had been chief make-up artist for the Moscow State Theatre but came to America to seek his fortune. He arrived in Los Angeles in 1908 and his entrance was so perfectly timed to bring him fame and fortune that it must have been scripted by Fate. Hollywood in those days was a place of orange groves and dusty, unpaved roads, the cinema was in its infancy, and so was the whole cosmetics industry. A film actress would make up her face for the camera with petroleum jelly powdered with flour, or with cold cream dusted with cornstarch, or, at the very best, with a crudely coloured greasepaint stick which went on like a thick mask. It was all very primitive, but on the other hand some sort of make-up was necessary because the crude carbon lighting of those early films did the oddest things to faces: freckles and skin blemishes photographed black, so did gold teeth or fillings; pink cheeks came out a dirty grey and skin, a deathly white. Factor's first breakthrough was something called Supreme Greasepaint which he launched on the film world, along with his eyeshadows and pencils, in 1914. This greasepaint came in several colours, was in cream form, and packaged in a tube: it was the forerunner of today's foundation cream.

Clara Bow was impulsive, modern, wild —all that a twenties flapper aspired to.

75

In the early days before the great Hollywood studios became more costume-conscious, it was the faces of the stars that had the most impact on the public, and it was Max Factor who most often had the task of grooming them into beauty. 'From Mary Pickford onwards,' proclaimed a newspaper article in the early thirties, 'he found film faces for them all. He has made more plain girls beautiful than any man living.'

Among early Max Factor clients were Hollywood's first box office successes, the two smouldering vamps, Theda Bara and Pola Negri. They blackened their eyelids, used mascara, and persuaded ordinary girls to try eye make-up for the very first time. There was Mary Pickford, the innocent-looking beauty whose blonde ringlets and sweet face earned her the title of The World's Sweetheart—and an annual salary more than that of America's President Woodrow Wilson.

But it was Clara Bow in the early twenties who became the first screen star to conjure up the whole spirit of her time. Clara Bow was the blue-print for the Flapper—she was impulsive, modern, wild. She drank and smoked, and her untidy bobbed hair, Cupid's bow mouth, large eyes and pencilled brows were what all young women soon aspired to. Max Factor increased the fullness of her lower lip 'to make a more provocative mouth' and taught her that by holding her head down and looking up

Above: Max Factor photographed with one of his most famous clients, Jean Harlow. His technique and the cosmetics he created for the Hollywood stars made him a household name.

at the camera, it would accentuate the whites of her eyes and make them look larger.

For Mae Murray, another twenties star, he devised what the publicity men nicknamed 'beestung lips', but this gimmick seems to have ended rather sourly. 'Mae Murray's own personality,' said a press report later, 'has been completely shrouded by the publicity given her famous lips.'

Below: Theda Bara, known as 'The Vamp', was an early Max Factor star.

In 1928 another Max Factor star, Jean Harlow, had her eyebrows plucked into a thin line, and her hair dyed platinum blonde. The ripples this caused among women are reflected in the beauty editors' columns of the time. In answer to dozens of readers' queries, they advised putting ether on the brows to ease the pain of plucking away the eyebrows, and to massage the head with warm oil to counteract the dryness and splitting hair that was an inevitable result of such drastic bleaching. Blondes were popular until 1938, but then the appearance of the lovely Hedy Lamarr had everyone reaching for the black dye, including her fellow stars. For if one Hollywood studio came up with a winner, rival studios desperately tried to force their girls into the same mould: Marlene Dietrich was first brought to Hollywood to be a second Greta Garbo.

Joan Crawford went through a number of looks, including the Hedy Lamarr. She started as a saucer-eyed pin-up in the twenties, but became most famous for the way in which she over-lipsticked her big square mouth, which in turn was copied by later stars in the thirties and forties. Max Factor once said he used to tease Crawford about the thickness with which she applied her make-up. 'But Mr Factor,' she used to protest, 'I've got to hide those freckles.' Max Factor transformed the young Judy Garland, and he groomed Rita Cansino, a brunette with a low forehead which he plucked to make more attractive. Later her hair was dyed red and she became famous as Rita Hayworth.

The star-struck public were greedy for tips on how to do all this for themselves; and they devoured the intimate glimpses they were given into the beauty habits of their favourites. From the twenties until the War, beauty columns were full of 'The Secrets of the Stars' kind of hints. The best of them was delivered in typical fashion by Mae West. When a columnist asked her how she kept her eyes so bright, she drawled in her famous low voice: 'I make a point of using them.' Describing how she put cleansing cream on in the bath so that the steam would help it work, she added as an afterthought, 'When you finally take it off, your face feels as clean as a chorus girl's conscience.'

Jean Harlow had this warning for her admirers: 'Very few people who admire blonde hair realize that every little speck of dust or grime appears on the surface as clearly as it would on a white dress or coat.' Platinum hair, she said, had to be shampooed every night; and she let slip that the product she used to make her own hair shiny was Brillox. Carole Lombard admitted that she had on her dressing table three creams, two lipsticks, two rouges (one for day and one for evening), two boxes of powder, one puff, one facepowder brush, eyeshadow, eyebrow pencil, eyelash make-up and a make-up blender to smooth over arms and shoulders. Ginger Rogers suggested that girls should flick their eyebrows upwards at the outward corners to give themselves a wide-awake look.

Nothing was too banal or silly to make good copy. Max Factor himself revealed that the 'lips of Greta Garbo must be especially made up after her kissing scenes for the screen.' This,

Platinum blondes were all the rage until Hedy Lamarr arrived on the scene in 1938. She wore her glossy black hair parted in the middle and was imitated just as slavishly by other stars as she was by the public. Even Joan Crawford (*inset*) managed to achieve a good likeness, though she was later to say, 'Everyone copied my fuller mouth, darker eyebrows. But I wouldn't copy anybody. If I can't be me I don't want to be anybody.'

Left: Greta Garbo gained such a vast following among the public that rival studios were eager to try and cash in on her looks. *Below*: During the War, Veronica Lake and her peek-a-boo hair style that she was asked to change before it caused accidents among her young fans working in wartime factories.

he said, was because Garbo was a 'heavyweight kisser' unlike Mae West, who was a 'lightweight kisser whose powder and rouge are hardly disturbed by her romantic moments before cameras.'

Right at the beginning, Max Factor shrewdly put his more successful products onto the market for all women to buy. He called his commercial cosmetic line Society Make-up, so that women would not be scared off by too unladylike and showbiz an image. But he still used his stars to illustrate the leaflets he distributed to the public: young Bette Davies demonstrated how to put on powder, Ginger Rogers dabbed on rouge, and Myrna Loy painted her lips. He was particularly proud that none of them asked for money in exchange for endorsing his products.

Max Factor died in 1938. He was the first and only make-up artist to have won an Academy of Motion Picture Arts and Sciences Award. He had just written the epitaphs for the Vamp and the Platinum Blonde, the two types of beauty he had helped so much to make popular. 'We used to admire the artificial woman and the sophisticated woman of fashion. What we want now is the outdoor girl.'

In the thirties the great costume designers of Hollywood came into their own. It was a most elegant period for film clothes, partly because some designers were recruited from the

Right: Marlene Dietrich was originally intended to be another Garbo, but took off as a star in her own right.

outside world of haute couture, and partly because the new talking movies meant that stars had, literally, to dress more quietly than they had in the past. Soft velvets, crepes, and wools that draped and clung became popular, because the taffetas and rustling satins of the previous decade made too much noise on the new soundtracks. Jewellery was cut down because anything too extravagant clanked audibly. Several of the great thirties' stars were noted for their elegance, and when these heroines swapped the hard, boyish lines of the twenties for the more feminine, bias-cut, figure-hugging dresses of the new decade, it encouraged the public to change too. When the designer Adrian put Joan Crawford in broad, padded shoulders in an effort to make her hips look smaller, he undoubtedly helped make this silhouette the favourite it became throughout the second half of the thirties, and all through the forties. Joan Crawford was named 'The Most Imitated Woman in the World' in 1932 and in 1937. In 1934 that distinction went to Marlene Dietrich, whom Travis Banton, an ex-couture designer, had helped to make as immaculate as any fashion plate.

But of all the thirties stars, it was Greta Garbo who most captured the public imagination. Cecil Beaton, who adored this strange, shy star, wrote, 'Her clothes, which are never of the feminine fluffy kind (in fact she possesses no evening dress) have real elegance. She buys them from the local Army and Navy store, where workmen, sailors and the like come for overalls and sweat shirts. Lipstick and nail varnish are put to shame by her; she uses no make-up save a dark line like a symbol on her eyelids . . . a symbol which only instinct created and yet which the world has copied.' Eye make-up was not the only fashion Garbo inspired. In 1932 in the film *Romance*, Adrian put her in a little hat tipped saucily over one eye—and for the rest of the decade that is how women wore their hats. When Garbo was photographed in private life wearing a beret, berets broke out on millions of heads.

It was in the thirties that producers first persuaded great Paris designers to turn their hands to film clothes, but on the whole these stints were not particularly successful. Coco Chanel was lured to Hollywood by Samuel Goldwyn in 1932. She dressed

In the forties and fifties Hollywood had a profound effect on women's shapes. Pin-up pictures unashamedly showed off the stars' vital statistics. Rita Hayworth (*right*) was a favourite wartime sex symbol, but in the fifties it was Marilyn Monroe's even more exaggerated curves that were admired, and a whole host of busty blondes emerged in imitation of her. Jayne Mansfield and Diana Dors (*below*) emphasised their bosoms as far as was anatomically and technically possible.

Gloria Swanson in *Tonight or Never*, and left soon afterwards. The *New Yorker* commented: 'They told her her dresses weren't sensational enough. She made a lady look like a lady. Hollywood wants a lady to look like two ladies!' Six years later Elsa Schiaparelli was invited to design some film clothes for Mae West. Miss West sent a tailor's dummy made up to her measurements to Paris, but when the clothes arrived they did not fit properly and a lot of time was wasted on alterations.

In the forties, screen fashions like world fashions, were seriously blighted by shortages and restrictions. They became cruder; but in those war years, the pin-up flourished as though to compensate for the glamour lacking in other areas. Betty Grable was the most famous of all, admired for her beautiful 'million-dollar' legs, and soldiers' requests for her picture ran to as many as 20,000 a week. Dorothy Lamour, best-known for the exotic and revealing sarongs she had worn in films in the late thirties, continued to be a popular sex-symbol, and caused a vogue for tropical prints that lasted all through the War. Rita Hayworth, her hair dyed red, was christened 'The Goddess of Love of the Twentieth Century', and became immensely popular as a pin-up. Her photograph is supposed to have been taped to the atom bomb that was dropped on Hiroshima. Lana Turner posed in figure-hugging jumpers and became known as 'The Sweater Girl'. This gave the knitwear industry a nice boost, though hers was but a mild foretaste of the kind of figure that was to dominate the fifties.

Hollywood's wartime hairstyles were mostly long, but they were inventive and influential: perhaps because hair was one of the few areas left in which a woman could express her femininity. Bette Davies's sausage-roll style was popular, as were Betty Grable's saucy topknot of curls and Rita Hayworth's glossy waves (the first to be set on big rollers). But it was Veronica Lake's sultry over-one-eye style that caused the greatest stir. It was copied so widely that she was asked by the U.S. War Manpower Commission to change it before it caused ghastly accidents by tangling up her imitators in factory machinery. Her obliging comment: 'Any girl who wears her hair over one eye is silly. I certainly don't, except in pictures.'

In the dawn of the fifties the studios were still nervous of the censors, and the big busts of Jane Russell and Marilyn Monroe had to be kept in check. Their dresses were lined with wire so that no matter what antics they got up to, their breasts never wobbled. But in a film called *The French Line*, released in 1954, Jane Russell appeared in a blatantly vulgar costume. It was a kind of swimsuit that pushed her breasts as far up and out as anatomically possible, and it even had saucy holes cut in it to reveal parts of the stomach and hips. From that moment on, there was no restraining the vital statistics of the stars. Marilyn Monroe had the added advantage of having weak ankles and crooked legs which meant her buttocks swayed when she walked and she insisted on exaggerating this by always wearing skin tight skirts. Monroe was copied as avidly by other would-

Joan Crawford was originally put into square-shouldered dresses in an attempt to make her hips look slimmer, and she helped to boost a fashion that endured until after the War. In 1932 she was named The Most Imitated Woman in the World.

The teenager was invented in America and it was Hollywood who introduced her to the world with stars like Elizabeth Taylor (*below*) and Audrey Hepburn (*left*) who had an instant effect on the way young girls looked.

be sex bombshells as by the public. Paler imitations like Mamie von Doren, Jayne Mansfield, Diana Dors and Anita Ekberg all helped to put the women of the world into uplift bras, waist-cinching belts and pencil skirts.

Perhaps the last powerful influence that Hollywood had was on the way young people dressed. The teenager had been invented in America and it was the American cinema who introduced her to the world in the fifties. There were sweet-faced stars like the young Elizabeth Taylor, whose bubble-cut hair and dark eyebrows became all the rage; the *gamine* Audrey Hepburn, whose urchin hair-cut and defined brows caused a sensation along with her clothes in films like *Sabrina* and *Roman Holiday*; and of course there was Grace Kelly, whose cool blonde beauty was greatly admired. Soon the screen seemed to be filled with wholesome kids (Debbie Reynolds and Sandra Dee were typical) in ponytails and gingham frocks.

Right: Later in the fifties, wholesome all-American kids like Sandra Dee (*left*) became popular. But across the Atlantic the European cinema was producing a new and altogether earthier type of star, epitomized by Sophia Loren.

But this was Hollywood's final fling. The European cinema had been steadily gaining ground throughout the fifties and new stars sprung up who had more and more influence on fashion and beauty. The European girls were altogether earthier and more real. In France the adorable, kittenish Brigitte Bardot took the teenage look, but made it sexy instead of merely cute. A little later, Catherine Deneuve became the model for all young French women who aspired to be chic. In Italy a regiment of well-built young women emerged—Gina Lollobrigida, Sophia Loren, Anna Magnani and Silvano Mangano. They favoured backcombed hair, blackened eyes, pale lips, and went in for wearing soaking wet shirts that clung to their maternal breasts (there always seemed to be a good excuse for this) or skirts hitched up to reveal sturdy thighs. In England we produced our own star cast in the new mould—Julie Christie, who played the part of a model girl in *Darling* (1965)—and, as models were the new heroines of the day, doubled her impact.

Remembering the old influential days of Hollywood, mighty publicity campaigns are launched from time to time to promote the fashions of certain films. Sometimes they work. Faye Dunaway's Thirties wardrobe for *Bonnie and Clyde* certainly relaunched the beret and the cardigan. But women audiences are notoriously unpredictable and very often it is the totally unexpected in a film which succeeds in setting a trend. Maria Schneider's frizzy hair in *Last Tango in Paris* revived the perm in a way that no deliberate campaign could have engineered more successfully. In general though, the public, as a Hollywood publicity man said sadly not so long ago, are 'more on Jackie Onassis than on movies and movie stars nowadays'.

The cinema's influence on our looks has declined, but occasionally a film still launches a new fashion. Faye Dunaway's thirties wardrobe for *Bonnie and Clyde* made berets and sweaters popular (*right*), and Maria Schneider's frizzed hair in *Last Tango in Paris* gave the permanent wave a whole new lease of life.

7 Freedom Fighters

Men, it is true, have given us most of this century's fashions, but all along it has been women who have tried to make our lives a little easier. Once in a while, when clothes have got out of hand, a woman designer has taken fashion by its elegant neck and given it a good shake until all its complications, restrictions and fussiness have fallen away. Chanel did it twice, once in the twenties and again in the fifties. Mary Quant did it for young people in the late fifties and early sixties. Biba had a sideways crack at it later on in that decade, and in Italy Nanni Strada is trying to do it again today.

Gabrielle Chanel could not understand why anyone should expect men to be able to design clothes for women, and she had the greatest contempt for her male colleagues in the fashion business. 'They don't understand the importance of a beautiful long neck, the need to emphasize the length of the leg, to make shoulders just so . . . to make the jacket so you can raise your arms.' Being a woman, and an energetic and lively one at that, Chanel did understand and she prided herself above everything on her ability to make clothes that 'women can live in, breathe in, feel comfortable in, and look young in.' She has been named 'the inventor of twentieth-century woman' because at a time when others were obsessed with silks and satins and feathers and lace and all sorts of frivolous nonsense, Chanel dared to sell simple jackets and waistless dresses in plain cloths. 'In 1916,' says her most recent biographer, 'she made such decisive changes in fashion that she compelled it to change centuries.'

A photograph of Chanel taken in the South of France in the twenties shows her in an outfit that would look good today: navy sailor trousers, a navy blue jumper, rows of pearls round her neck and a navy blue beret on her head. It is almost impossible to believe that barely ten years earlier, women had been struggling about in long skirts and picture hats. At first Chanel's was called the 'Poor Look' because it was so understated and because the fabrics she chose—jersey, flannel, tweed—looked so drab. Designer Paul Poiret, a rival whose once-bright star was fading when Chanel's was in the ascendency, described it cynically as 'poverty de luxe'. That was nearer the mark, for the secret of the Chanel look was to wear the plainest garment and then pile on to it a mass of costume jewellery (you could use the real stuff she said, so long as it was so extravagant it looked like junk) along with other well-thought-out accessories which gave the outfit richness and glamour without altering its basic simplicity. Chanel taught us the lesson we dress by today: that

Left: Quant photographed with her husband Alexander Plunket Greene in the early sixties. She is wearing one of her own typically pared-down dresses. *Overleaf:* Coco Chanel, the greatest designer of all. Here, she is wearing her favourite colour combination of black and white.

91

the clothes themselves are less important than what you put with them and how you wear them. It was she who invented what fashion editors are fond of calling 'The Total Look'.

Chanel was a beautiful, vivid woman with flaring nostrils and fire in her black eyes. She was her own best advertisement, and wore her clothes with more flair and dash than even the richest or most elegant of her customers. When she was over eighty years old women still wanted to look like her, and now, six years after her death, Chanel's ideas are still part of our lives, and they always will be. It was she who launched in 1920 the first non-floral fragrance, Chanel No. 5. It was she who first showed how elegant a plain black dress could be, how crisp a white shirt or collar looks with a dark outfit. She taught how flattering spectacles can be if their frames are in horn or tortoise-shell, how charming a white gardenia looks pinned to the lapel, how comfortable a cardigan jacket feels, and how effective it is to wear lots of chains and pearls round the neck instead of just one. She stressed the importance of keeping hair simple and glossy, and in desperation she would sometimes take the scissors to her customers' hair herself, chopping off the rigid waves put in by hairdressers. Her model girls were the first to wear their hair tied back simply at the nape of the neck with a black bow, a style for which lots of us are thankful today.

Of all the fashions she gave us, the suntan is the one we probably most appreciate. Chanel liked the open air and was active and healthy. In 1920 she bought her first holiday house in the sun of the South of France and there she let her already swarthy skin tan even browner. Soon it became all the rage, so much so that Quentin Bell wrote, 'The great innovation of the century has been the adoption of a new standard of beauty in pigmentation. Hitherto the ideal had been one of shaded and unfreckled fairness; sunburn was felt to imply a healthy industrious open-air life, tolerable perhaps in a man, but not in a lady. But in the twenties, the woman who could prove that she was no city worker, but one of those able to bask in the sunlight of the Mediterranean, was esteemed for her tan just as her grandmother had been for her pallor. Thus we find the rare spectacle of women powdering themselves brown when unable to roast themselves to the same end.'

This extraordinary woman, whose influence still endures, had the most miserable start in life imaginable. Chanel herself never told the truth about it, preferring to dream up picturesque or touching stories which she changed to suit her audience. The truth was more dramatic than anything she could invent. She was born illegitimate and in a poorhouse, the daughter of a travelling peddler and his long-suffering unhappy woman Jeanne, whom he finally consented to marry when she found herself pregnant for the third time. When Jeanne Chanel died, Gabrielle was twelve, her father deposited her in a grim orphanage run by nuns and then vanished. There she spent six years. She then found work as a seamstress in the French provincial town of Moulins. In Moulins she acquired the nickname

Coco, by which she was known all her life. She had taken a job as a singer in a café—anything to get out of the rut of poverty—and one of the only songs she knew was an old favourite '*Qui qu'a vu Coco dans L'Trocadero?*' ('Who has seen Coco in the Trocadero?'). When the audience wanted more they stamped and shouted '*Coco . . . Coco . . .*'

She was not a success as a singer, but it was in Moulins that she found her saviour, a wealthy cavalry officer called Etienne Balsan. Coco lived with him for three years, and he helped her to open a hat shop in his bachelor flat in the Boulevard Malesherbes in Paris. He also introduced her to Arthur Capel, always known as 'Boy', a polo-playing Englishman. Chanel loved him fiercely until his death in a car crash in 1919. It was Boy Capel who set her up in her own shop in the Rue Cambon, another in Deauville, and another in Biarritz. At first it was only hats she sold, but she soon added clothes, and before Boy's death she was able to pay him back all his investment.

Chanel used her past, she made it work for her. The early bleak years had given her a taste for simplicity, even austerity, and other memories cropped up in her clothes all the time. Black and white, her favourite colour combination, echoed the habits of the nuns at the orphanage; the smock tops she liked to make were similar to those of the schoolchildren she knew long years before, and the pristine white shirt she always favoured was like her old school uniform; the braid with which she loved to trim her suits adorned the cavalry officers' uniforms in Moulins; and the craze for all things English—sweaters, tweeds, tailoring—came from her association with Boy Capel. Her memories served her well.

Once she became established, Chanel's friends were the most interesting people in Paris. From Colette to Jean Cocteau, she knew them all, and her lovers were noble and rich men, among them the Grand Duke Dimitri of Russia (one of the assassins of the sinister monk Rasputin) and Bendor, Duke of Westminster and the richest man in England. Her feuds were equally celebrated. In the thirties she was particularly piqued by the success of the new designer Elsa Schiaparelli, whose eccentric clothes were the most talked about in Paris. It looked as though she had stolen Chanel's limelight as well as some of her best customers, and Chanel loathed her for it. She had her own devious ways of punishing people who fraternized with the enemy. Chanel once caught the photographer Horst lunching with Schiaparelli in the Ritz. She approached their table smiling sweetly and Horst, of course, rose politely to his feet to greet her. Then Chanel went into action—and kept him talking for one solid hour without addressing a single word to her rival. Horst's torture only ended when he muttered something about being late for an appointment and rushed from the hotel, his lunch forgotten. She usually had a quarrel simmering with Mrs Reginald Fellowes, who had once been her most famous client but later favoured Schiaparelli. Both Chanel and Daisy Fellowes had houses in the South of France, and once, during a

Chanel photographed in 1964. By now her second fashion revolution was in full swing and the cardigan suit and jewellery she is wearing had again become the smart woman's uniform.

lull in hostilities, Mrs Fellowes asked Chanel's house guests over from Rocquebrune for lunch and a swim in her pool. They arrived but then declined to swim—Mrs Fellowes' swimming instructor had a pink rash on his chest and they thought it might be catching. Mrs Fellowes had to admit that she had made the poor fellow shave his chest because it upset her to see the hair on it floating about under water.

Chanel was also obstinate. In the sixties the *Sunday Times* wished to present her with an award for her unique services to fashion. Chanel refused to cross the Channel for the presentation at the London Hilton Hotel although the whole fashion world was to attend. Charming young men were dispatched to Paris to persuade her. Each time she would agree to come—and then change her mind the moment they left. In the end she did stay away, to the crushing disappointment of fans like myself. I did see her once, though, crouched in the shadows at the top of the stairs in her *salon* in the Rue Cambon, watching, as she always did, her new collection being paraded before the press and buyers.

Chanel closed down her successful business before the outbreak of the Second World War, and remained in seclusion for fifteen years. Everyone thought she had retired for good, but she decided to re-open in 1954 at the age of seventy-one. By then women were wearing pencil slim skirts that reached to mid-calf and were difficult to walk in. Wasp waists, too, were the fashion and Chanel thought these an exaggeration 'even on a wasp'. The fashion world wondered how on earth the old girl dared hope to revive her pre-war ideas and have any success at all. That first comeback collection was a nightmare for Chanel. The audience viewed it in stony silence, and she was panned in the press: 'Ghosts of the 1930's gowns,' they said. Within a year they were eating their words, women were back in her cardigan suits—Chanel had liberated them all over again. Rich women queued up to buy them from Chanel herself, others had a choice among the myriad copies that appeared at every price.

One thing Coco Chanel scorned, and that was the way designers change fashion every season, seemingly just for the sake of it. She never did, and was not ashamed to wear the same uniform for years and years—an easy skirt, a cardigan jacket with pockets she could stuff her hands into, a white shirt as the perfect background for her strings of pearls and chains. 'I love only old clothes. Old clothes are like old friends.'

Ask Mary Quant who her heroine is and without hesitation she will answer—Coco Chanel. She will probably do more and tell you about the thrill she felt when she occasionally lunched in the Paris Ritz and found herself only a few paces from Chanel, and how she still regrets that shyness prevented her from speaking to the great designer. Mary does not hide the fact that the admiration was not mutual, and laughs when she tells how an American journalist asked Chanel, 'Do you know that Mary Quant in England thinks you're the greatest designer in the world?' 'Coming from Mary Quant,' replied Chanel icily, 'that is very small praise.' At the same time Quant was compared with Chanel by Eugenia Sheppard, the fashion reporter of the *Herald Tribune*. Although at first it was hard to see that the ultra-modern ex-art student had much in common with the aged star who clothed the richest women in the world, it is true that Quant and Chanel shared the belief that clothes should be without fuss, and that The Total Look was the one that mattered.

The revolution that Mary Quant initiated in the late fifties and early sixties was no less far-reaching in its way than the ones Chanel inspired twice in her lifetime. Chanel invented the twentieth-century woman; Quant invented the girl.

For more than half of this century it was the mature, elegant woman who was admired in fashion. It was actually said that 'a woman doesn't learn to dress well until she is over thirty-five'. The mature woman was the one the dressmakers catered for, perhaps for the very good reason that you needed a mature husband's cheque book to pay for the jewels, the furs, and the workmanship of couture clothes. Even as recently as in the fifties our ideal was the sophisticate; looking back, how *old* all the model girls looked in those days. In fact, it didn't seem to matter how aged you were, and Consuelo Vanderbilt (Mrs Jacques Balsan) was elected to the Fashion Hall of Fame when she was in her late seventies.

When I was a teenager in the mid-fifties, all my clothes were versions of what my mother or elder sister wore; everything, that is, apart from a pair of pedal-pusher jeans and a gingham skirt inspired by Brigitte Bardot. There was no real style for a girl of my age, no make-up, no hair styles, and on the whole, the clothes that were available made a teenager look either years older than she really was, or years younger. Then along came Mary Quant.

She was a high-spirited creature, who had studied art at the Goldsmith's College, and her boyfriend was a tall, gangling, aristocratic young man called Alexander Plunket Greene. They were both very much part of the Chelsea set: a group of young things who had broken away from the values of their parents and preferred to dress in sweaters and jeans, admired anything to do with jazz music or art, and spent their time in coffee bars or cellar jazz clubs, at wild parties or cooking up wicked pranks. Mary and Alexander and some friends once staged an elaborate kidnap scene in London to see what passers by would do if they saw a girl abducted into a passing car. It ended with them fleeing in terror when the all-too-real police arrived.

Like all couples in their group, they were constantly short of cash (Alexander seemed to zip through his monthly allowance on the day it arrived), but full of ideas. The one that led to their fame and fortune was not unique, but the difference was that they actually *did* it—by opening a boutique selling the kind of clothes and accessories they liked. At first there was no question of Mary designing anything for it herself: her job was to be the buyer for the shop. The trouble was that she couldn't

Overleaf: Mary Quant was one of the first women to try Vidal Sassoon's new geometric cut. Sassoon himself clips her fringe.

find anything she liked enough to buy, and in the end she was forced to knuckle down and produce her own ideas. She bought a sewing machine and some Butterick patterns, which she adapted by chopping some bits off and adding others. She bought some cloth in Harrods because she didn't know about buying it wholesale. The dresses she made were short and skinny, the shapes were simple—pinafores and tunics, neat jackets and pleated skirts—and she made them in unexploited fabrics like flannel. For the windows of their shop, Mary accessorized the dresses in her own uninhibited way and put them on dummies she had designed herself. Soon the place was stopping the traffic in the Kings Road.

The word about Bazaar got round fast. I remember the shock and delight with which it was greeted by a young audience who knew that this was exactly what they had been waiting for. Mary Quant's customers looked quite unlike anyone else at the time. They wore her exciting pared-down clothes with short straight hair, cut by Vidal Sassoon to swing like curtains on either side of their faces. They used whitish lipstick and lots of black around their eyes, wore black tights and boots, and heads would turn in the street to stare.

The clothes were not especially cheap; I fell in love with a plain grey flannel suit and the only way I could afford it was by begging a friend who sewed in Mary Quant's workroom to 'borrow' the pattern and make it up for me at home.

'No designer is ever responsible for such a revolution,' is Mary Quant's modest appraisal today. 'I just happened to start when that "something in the air" was coming to the boil. The clothes I made happened to fit in exactly with the teenage trend, with pop records and espresso bars and jazz clubs.'

But Quant's name went into fashion history. Wearing her kind of clothes proved that you were 'US'—part of what the Americans called the Youthquake—and not 'them', the squares, the fuddy-duddies, the older generation. Mary's combination of innocence and daring enabled her to plunge boldly into the fashion jungle, tearing down the old taboos as she blazoned her path. 'Why not?' was the standard reply to any sort of critical question in those days, and 'Why not?' was Mary's creed. It had never been done before, but why not make raincoats in shiny PVC, combine outrageous colours, or put spots with stripes and checks with spots? Why not shorten skirts, put girls in football sweaters, braces, knickerbockers, crazy coloured tights and boxer shorts? Why not use evening fabrics for daytime and day fabrics for evening? Why not make furs fun?

She brought fashion alive. She put it in touch with what was going on in the world, and with the young. And when she had done this for clothes she turned her attention to foundation garments and cosmetics, giving us the lightest underclothes ever, and a range of make-up which included unheard-of things like highlighters, glossers and face-shapers.

In 1966, Quant was awarded the O.B.E. Towards the end of the sixties, she and Alexander began closing down their

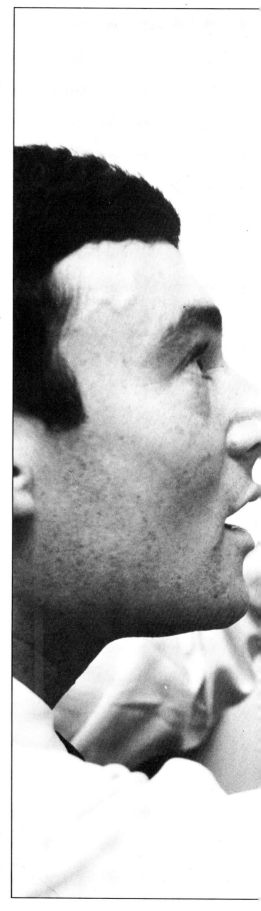

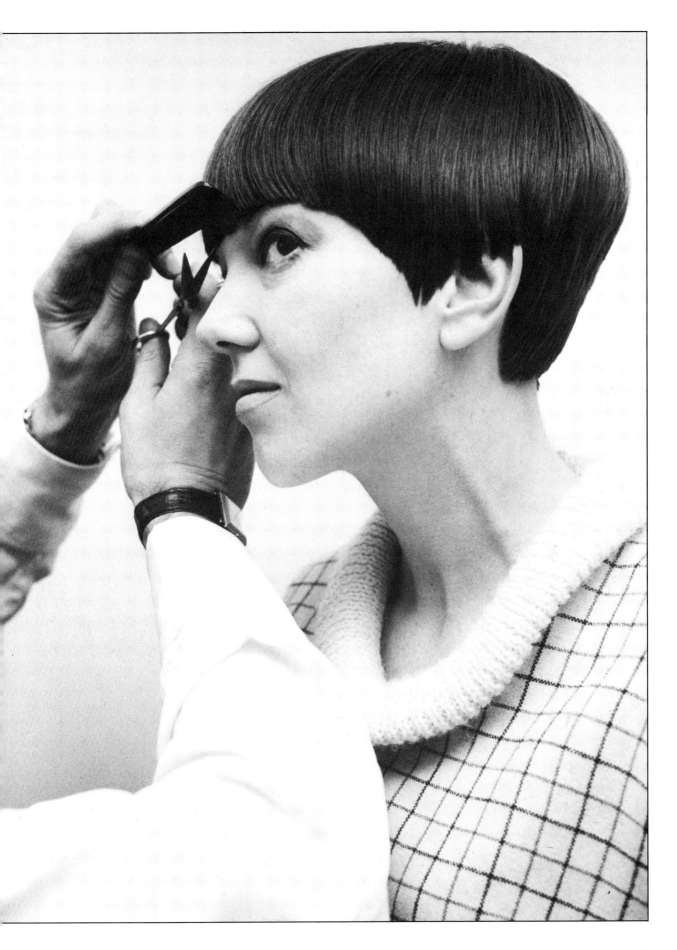

boutiques. Her name was bigger business now, and it was appearing on footwear, swimsuits, dress patterns, and later, on writing paper and wine. Ten years after her revolution Mary Quant had become part of the British Establishment. The post-Quant generation, the 15-year-olds of the second half of the sixties, now needed to find themselves a new heroine. They soon did—in Biba.

Gentle, beautiful Barbara Hulanicki was well-known for her fashion illustrations, but in 1964 she decided to change horses and to make clothes instead of drawing them. She called herself Biba (it was her younger sister's nickname) and went into business. At first she trod gently, designing one-off things: a crepe skirt, a simple little gingham dress, a towelling robe. She persuaded newspaper fashion editors to feature them on their pages as mail-order items, and Barbara, with her husband, Fitz, despatched them to readers by post from their own flat. The clothes were so young, so cheap and so successful that the orders they received nearly swamped them. Even Barbara's mother was put to work sewing skirts to meet the demand. They decided to put their business on a more professional basis, by investing in a proper shop and bringing out later a new kind of mail-order catalogue. The tiny boutique they opened sold the same sort of simple, inexpensive clothes, plus some amusing accessories, and soon girls were queueing outside. On busy days customers were stripping off and trying things on in the street. Barbara and Fitz were forced to move to bigger premises. They and the shop assistants pushed the dress rails hung with clothes along the pavements to their new shop in Kensington Church Street, a colourful informal place with old-fashioned stands full of felt hats and feather boas, and the first communal changing room.

Biba's designs, even the tee-shirts she made fashionable, were hall-marked by their narrow little shoulders or cut-away armholes. She maintained that if you looked narrow across the top then you looked narrow all over, and these designs suited the new Twiggy shape of girl to perfection. The Biba customer was utterly unlike the crisp Quant swinger. She had a waiflike body with thin shoulders and hollow chest, a pale face with huge, elaborately made-up eyes. Later on she grew more sophisticated and acquired blood-red lips and nails painted black. Her hair was frizzed into a pre-Raphaelite cloud, or worn in a knob on top with tendrils trailing around the face.

When Biba started her catalogue in 1967 she took the unconventional steps of choosing models who exaggerated this look, and allowing her photographers a free hand to do anything, so long as they got the look across in their pictures. Sarah Moon became the most famous of these: her misty, moody pictures for the Biba catalogue started a widespread craze in fashion photography which lasts to this day. Nothing like these unusual results had ever been seen before. The mail order business had always played it safe, and Biba's catalogue gave a new excitement and glamour to the old idea of shopping by post.

Mary Quant as she is today, nearly twenty years after her name first went into fashion history. *Inset:* An early eye-catching advertisement for Quant cosmetics – the model is Penelope Tree.

100

TO THE NAKED EYE IT'S A NAKED FACE.

Mary Quant's Starkers.
The make-up that looks like
it isn't there.
You can get it in three
semi-matt skin tones. Bare light.
Bare dark. Bare bronze.
And even if it's hiding
anything, it won't
look as though you have
anything to hide.
To the naked eye.

MARY QUANT

Left: A moody Sarah Moon picture for Biba. The model is Ingrid Boulting, now a film actress.
Above: Barbara Hulanicki in 1977.

In 1972 Barbara Hulanicki daringly took over the vast department store that had been Derry and Toms in Kensington. She now had the chance to apply her romantic, nostalgic (some said decadent) taste to all aspects of fashion and to household goods as well. Sheets in the new store were in dark brown or beige satin, lingerie harked back to the thirties, lampshades were heavily fringed or draped with lace shawls, palms and aspidistras stood about in Art Nouveau pots, and clothes drooped from curly hat stands. The counters were in black glass, the walls were dark, the lighting sombre. Stepping into that store was more like going to the theatre than shopping, the entire building looked like an elaborate exotic stage set, an uninhibited mixture of Art Deco and Art Nouveau, with some Victoriana thrown in for good measure.

Some customers loved it, but many pundits predicted disaster. Nothing like this had been tried before, and they said the Biba people seemed to be ignoring the basic economic principles by putting palm trees and sofas where they should have had more counters and some hard selling. No doubt nothing so outrageous will ever be tried again, for although Biba became the most talked-about place in town, the pundits were right and it was a financial disaster. Within three years the store had closed, and Barbara and her husband left to live in Brazil.

Nanni Strada's revolution is just beginning. Ten years after her training as a fashion designer in Italy, and in the middle of a successful though unspectacular career, Nanni Strada was in London preparing for the birth of her daughter when, she says, the scales suddenly fell from her eyes. It dawned on her that she utterly disagreed with almost every rule that the fashion business, which included herself, took for granted. Like Chanel she did not feel that fashion should change every season; she thought the business of making garments in different sizes ridiculously complicated, and she 'no longer wanted to design clothes that were a hollow mould for the human body'. She decided, in fact, that the only thing for her to do was leave the fashion business altogether.

That was in 1967. Nanni Strada was only twenty-six and resilient, and she chose instead, fortunately, to tramp round museums and archives in Britain and in Italy, learning all she could about Oriental clothing, which seemed the nearest expression of the fashion revolution she had in mind. She experimented, too, with different methods of cutting and constructing clothes, always searching for simpler and more sensible solutions to the age-old problem of making a flat piece of cloth fit a rounded figure.

Ever since she learned to hold a pencil she has been a compulsive designer. 'I drew everywhere and on everything,' she says, and admits that she became used to people commenting, 'This child will become somebody one day'. Yet her success has not come easily. In 1974 Nanni Strada entered a competition sponsored by President Ghaddafi of Libya to find a modern

Left: Nanni Strada wearing one of her own designs: a dress made from a single piece of cloth with no seams and only ties for fastening.

national costume for his country. Her design was a dress made of a single piece of cloth with no seams at all, and only some ties for fastening. Nanni Strada was pleased with it because it met all her self-imposed conditions: it fitted all sizes, it could be worn by anyone, of any age, it displayed the fabric perfectly, it could be packed flat and was therefore easy to distribute. But Miss Strada's dress did not win the contest, and what is more, when she defiantly tried to put the dress into production herself in Italy, she could not persuade any of the conventional manufacturers to take on anything so unorthodox. She turned her back on the rag trade and took her design to the household linen manufacturers; and it is the tablecloth and sheet people who now turn out the revolutionary dress which is 'aimed at all women and not just a sophisticated elite'.

In the meantime Miss Strada had made a film about her researches, *The Cape and the Skin*, which has been shown at the Milan Triennale and by the Cooper Hewlitt Museum in New York. Her workmanlike but clever designs (which now include jackets, skirts, pants, shirts and children's things as well as dresses) sell well in Italy now, but she is still innovating, still experimenting. 'I would like to see my clothes become the new classics' she says.

I have great faith in her, a girl who looks more like an earnest art student than anyone involved with the fly-by-night world of fashion. Perhaps it is because I have one of her Libyan dresses myself and every time I put it on I marvel at the ingenuity of the idea. It is so simple, so comfortable—one can't imagine why no one invented it years ago.

Overleaf: When Biba became a department store, Barbara Hulanicki had the opportunity to apply her taste to household goods as well as to fashion. Everything in this picture bears the Biba label.

104

Right: The first mail-order dress designed by Barbara Hulanicki, as it appeared in the *Daily Mirror* in 1964. As Biba grew the designs became more and more nostalgic. The droopy satin dress below, from a Biba catalogue, was typical. The model is Stephanie Farrow, sister of Mia.

8 Showing Off

When I was at my finishing school in Paris, one afternoon we were led by our chaperone, not to the usual museum or art gallery, but to the elegant grey and white Dior salons to watch a fashion show. Perhaps our teachers thought that young ladies like us should be helped to feel at home in the couture houses where we would, no doubt, one day buy our dresses. I knew though that I should never aspire to a Dior original, so I took more interest in the mannequins than the clothes. These girls intrigued me: they were so sure-footed, so aloof and unsmiling, spinning and turning and stepping out with such confidence and *panache*. It was better than the theatre. Since then, as a fashion writer, I have had to sit through hundreds of such shows but, for me, the mannequins have never lost their original fascination.

Show modelling is an art, and the girl who does it is almost as important as the designer she works for. She has the vital job of interpreting his ideas and presenting them to the audience. All the designer can do by that stage is to peek through a hole in the curtain to see how the viewers are reacting. Dior once said that his mannequins were his most vital helpers: 'their role can seem passive, but one should remember that the most beautiful dresses in the world can be, literally, wasted on air if they are worn by bad models.' A boring model can have the audience nodding off to sleep in no time, but a girl with presence, a great model, will bring the show alive, she will have the audience on the edges of their seats, and she will ensure that the fashions she wears are successful ones. Their faces are not of paramount importance, and a show model need not be pretty; some of the stars have been downright plain. The solemn-faced Dolores was Norman Hartnell's favourite. 'She had a way of walking sideways like a crab. I hired her on the spot when she came to see me before the war. She became the Queen Mother's favourite.' Christine Tidmarsh, who worked for Yves Saint Laurent when he first started, had an enormous mouth and a bad skin, but no one noticed. She would bound into the *salon* with such verve and energy, that when she spun round the hem of her skirt would catch all the front row journalists' notebooks and send them flying off their knees. Bronwen Pugh (now Lady Astor) was an untidy, sulky-looking girl but she made an overnight reputation for herself when she first modelled for Balmain in Paris. A reporter described her as 'that Welsh girl who drags a fur along the runway as if she had just killed it and was taking it home to her mate.'

Bettina, the great show model, photographed during a fitting in the *cabine* or changing room at Jacques Fath in Paris in 1950.

Left: Show models do not have to be pretty but they must have presence. Dolores went to work for Norman Hartnell before the Second World War and became the Queen Mother's favourite.

Below: Christine Tidmarsh had such energy that when she spun round, the hem of her skirt would flick all the front-row journalists' note-books off their knees.

The first designer to understand the model's potential was Lady Duff Gordon, whose dressmaking establishment, Lucile, flourished from the beginning of the century. In those days mannequins were looked on as menials, and considered not much better than wax dummies. They wore uncomfortable boned corsets, often reaching from bosom to knee, which meant they couldn't sit down all day. If they modelled evening dresses they had to put them, for decency's sake, over black satin undergarments that covered all exposed flesh. Lady Duff Gordon was as much of a tyrant as anyone else, but she was shrewd enough to realize what a more glamorous type of girl could do for her dresses. She kept an eye out for likely beauties wherever she went and had a knack for spotting winners. She groomed the girls she hired, gave them exotic names and refused to allow them to wear the black satin *maillots*. She was a theatrical woman and her mannequins appeared on a little stage, complete with grey chiffon curtains, while background music wafted from a tiny orchestra.

Lots of Lucile girls did well for themselves. When Lady Duff Gordon opened a branch of her dress business in New York before the First World War, both she and her haughty English models were taken up in a big way by the impresario Ziegfeld. He commissioned Lady Duff Gordon to design clothes for his extravagant Follies reviews, and he stole her best models and turned them into show girls. Dolores, a tall unsmiling beauty who had been discovered as an errand girl in London, took New York by storm in 1917 when she appeared in a specially written number. 'Probably the most sensational beauty to ever appear in the Follies,' said a reporter. Dolores left for Paris in 1923 where she married a millionaire.

Two other Lucile mannequins, Hebe and Sumurun, left her and went to work for Captain Molyneux when he opened his couture house in Paris just after the First World War. Sumurun apparently means 'Enchantress of the Desert' and it was the name Lady Duff Gordon chose for Vera Ashby (who came from nowhere more exotic than London) because of her jet black hair and oriental look. She was paid thirty-five shillings a week when she started.

Vera Ashby is now an old lady in London, and she remembers to this day the terror with which she gave in her notice to Lady Duff Gordon. 'You couldn't stand up against Madame, she was a real power. When she discovered I wanted to go and work for the Captain she took me between her finger and thumb, turned me round to face the door and said "You . . . whom I have treated like a sister—GO".'

In Paris she found that modelling was considered very fast and loose and no model girl was received in polite society. 'But the young men adored to be seen out with us. Many of my friends were these young titled men. . . . I amused them with my broken French. I was always out. Actually I would have much preferred a family life but all I had in Paris was a hotel bedroom, and a cheap one at that. I hated the position of the

Left: Sumurun in a Molyneux dress with a fan of ostrich feathers. 'I was once told that the only woman in the world who could handle a fan better than me was the Queen of Spain.' *Inset:* Sumurun dressed by Molyneux for the finale of a fashion show in Paris. The jewellery lit up, and she was accompanied by two little 'slave' children. *Below:* Edwina Prue was recruited by Jean Patou in New York to model in his Paris *salon.*

women like us. Most of the models were kept, or, as we used to say then, "looked after" by men. But I must say, I did have an extraordinary life—one night I'd be eating a tin of peas in my tiny hotel room, the next it would be caviar at Maxim's. Captain Molyneux loaned me clothes to go out in—it was a good advertisement for him.'

Sumurun became well-known—'the mystic mannequin' they called her in the papers. She puts this down less to her beauty—'Hebe was far better looking'—than to the fact that she was good at her job: 'I liked to interpret the dresses, act them, if you like.' When *The People* serialized her life story in 1930 they described her as no less than 'world famous'. One of her more sensational appearances was in the finale of a fashion show put on at a charity ball in Paris. 'Molyneux designed a slap-up Oriental thing for me. Underneath the tunic there were electric lights and a jewel in my turban lit up, and my earrings, too. Two little black children threw rose petals at my feet. Men in the audience ran and picked them up and kissed them—the petals I had walked on—imagine! Some of my young boy-friends were waiting at the end of the catwalk. One of them came up and—with my hand on my heart this is true—he gave me two boxes with diamonds and emerald jewellery in them. That kind of thing happened in those days.' No less spectacular was Sumurun's outfit for the finale of a fashion show put on at Olympia in 1923. It was the year that Tutankhamun's tomb had been discovered, and the whole world was Egypt mad. Moly-neux designed a kind of Pharaoh's robe in shimmering gold for Sumurun and she was again accompanied by two little 'slave' children. A group of ladies told her afterwards that they had travelled all the way from Bath just to see her.

Sumurun married twice and ended her career as the chief *vendeuse,* or sales woman, at Norman Hartnell where she looked after no less a customer than The Queen of England.

What took the social stigma out of modelling and transformed the girls into perfectly acceptable women, was an idea that came to designer Jean Patou in 1924. Patou's clothes were immensely popular among smart women, but he wasn't attracting as many American buyers as his rivals Chanel or Molyneux. It occurred to him that the answer might be to show his clothes on American girls instead of French ones. In this way, the Americans would be able to identify more easily with his designs. He advertized in the New York papers for girls who must be 'smart, slender, with well-shaped feet and ankles and refined of manner'. The selection was to be made by a jury in *Vogue*'s office, and Patou himself went over to America to take part.

Five hundred eager candidates turned up—Patou was only looking for three girls but he was persuaded to choose six.

Edwina Prue, now Baroness d'Erlanger, was the youngest and last of the girls to be chosen. She was seventeen years old, had just left convent school and was desperate for work—'the only career we were prepared for in those days was marriage'—when she bumped into an acquaintance in the street who told her that she had been selected to go to Paris with Jean Patou. It was no use anyone else applying, the friend warned, Monsieur Patou now had all the models he needed. Undaunted, Edwina Prue rushed home and telephoned all the big New York hotels until she found where the designer was staying. She made an appointment with a secretary and went along to his suite. The secretary thought at first that Miss Prue was a journalist seeking an interview, but when she heard her business she told her that the outlook was bleak. Monsieur had indeed finished his selection. But when Patou came into the room, she took pity on Edwina Prue and pushed her forward. 'Jean Patou looked at me—I was very blonde and thin with small feet—and said, "You are the typical American girl I am looking for." He was leaving for Paris next day and they couldn't draw up a contract with me because I was under age. I sent my mother a cable saying COME AT ONCE, but I didn't say why because I knew she wouldn't approve. When she arrived she was so taken aback that she signed the contract, and I left for Paris with the others.'

'American girls were so neat and clean looking in those days. I suppose we were very attractive. We wore pleated skirts and little sweaters on which we sewed white piqué collars and cuffs. We buffed our fingernails and put vaseline on our eyelids and wore pink silk stockings with black patent pumps. I had no idea that I had any looks because I had always been told I was hideous, but it had been instilled in me by my mother that I should at all times look my best. "You may meet your whole future on a station platform," she used to say. And as it turned out my husband did find me on a station platform.'

For the opening night of his show in Paris, when the now-famous Americans were to model for the first time, Patou introduced a little touch of showmanship: he sent all his mannequins out together to do a turn round the rooms wearing nothing but their brief cotton dressing gowns. There was laughter and applause from the audience and the new girls were rated a great success. Patou succeeded in his aim of drawing the American buyers, but he also gave the model a new status and importance by showing the world that he cared enough about the girls who showed his clothes to go all the way to America in search of the right ones. Miss Prue, by the way, modelled for Jean Patou for a little over six months. She was carefully chaperoned, barely went out and in any case was painfully shy. Then later she left to work on *Vogue*.

The first model agency was opened in London in 1928. It was the brain child of Sylvia Gollidge, a brown-eyed girl from Blackpool who stood five feet eleven inches tall and had insured her long blonde hair for £1,000. She had been modelling herself since the age of sixteen and was so successful that she could hardly cope with offers of work. At first she would pass them on to good-looking friends, but then she formed the shrewder idea of channelling them into an agency. The Lucie Clayton agency it was called, and it flourished under her guidance. It ran charm courses, and taught debs to curtsey, and of course it handled show models and, later, photographic girls. At one time Lucie Clayton had 4,000 girls on its books, but in 1950 the agency was sold to its present owners and Sylvia Gollidge went to live in Australia.

If you ask a middle-class, middle-aged British woman what models she can remember from the pre-War days, she will scrabble around in her mind and perhaps come up with the names of Dawn and Gloria. Dawn and Gloria were the stars of the Selfridge's shows, and in the early thirties they were undoubtedly the most famous models in Britain. Gordon Selfridge, the extraordinary American who opened the great Oxford Street store in 1909, had a tremendous flair for publicity and was constantly thinking up ideas that would keep the customers rolling in. One year he put famous society ladies in charge of all his counters: the Duchess of Rutland was Ribbons, the Lady Farquhar was Lampshades, Lady Tree was Handkerchiefs and the Countess of Dudley was Stationery. But what the shoppers loved best were his fashion shows, in which Dawn and Gloria starred. Gordon Selfridge had a reputation for being able to manipulate anything, even the weather, to suit his own ends, and in 1932 he did just that. The summer was hot and fine and Selfridge arranged a Holiday Beach Parade on the roof of his store. Dawn and Gloria caused a sensation 'baring their limbs in the new wave wear', and made all the popular papers. On yet another occasion Mr Selfridge arranged for Gaumont British

Dawn (left) and Gloria (right), the two famous British models who were the stars of the Selfridge fashion shows in the thirties.

Christian Dior's favourite mannequins.
Above: Lucky. *From left to right:* Renée
Breton, wearing the New Look ('She is
good taste itself,' Dior once said), France
and Tania. *Opposite:* Alla.

films to hold their Miss England contest in his store. He installed a machine said to register the amount of IT (sex appeal) in any personality—Gloria registered 95 per cent. In an American poll Dawn was once voted the girl with the best figure in the world. Then in 1936 Dawn and Gloria left Selfridges to start a modelling school together.

In February 1947, in the elegant Paris *salon* of a new designer called Christian Dior, fashion was re-born again after the War years of austerity and utility. Dior's collection was wildly extravagant and so utterly unlike the plain practical clothes women had worn for the last eight years that it was known as The New Look. It caused a sensation in that grey post-War world.

Among the audience at this momentous fashion occasion was Bettina Ballard of *Vogue*, who felt, as soon as she stepped into his *salon*, that the new boy was up to something. 'I was conscious of an electric tension that I had never before felt in the couture. Suddenly all the confusion subsided, everyone was seated, and there was a moment of hush that made my skin prickle. The first girl came out, stepping fast, switching with a provocative swinging movement, whirling in the close-packed room, knocking over ashtrays with the strong flare of her pleated skirt and bringing everyone to the edges of their seats. After a few more costumes had passed all at the same exciting tempo, the audience knew that Dior had created a new look. . . . We were witness to a revolution in fashion and to a revolution in showing fashions as well.'

John Fairchild of *Women's Wear Daily* said that afterwards 'it was enough to say "Dior" anywhere in the world. Women got hysterical. Cash registers rang.' Soon Dior was selling one and a half times more clothes than the rest of the Paris designers put together, and his name had become by far the best known of all the designers. Every season, until his death in 1958, Dior continued to dictate what women would wear.

With all eyes centered on his *salon* for so long, it is not surprising that the girls he chose to show his clothes became famous in their turn. Dior's mannequins were important to him. He once explained, 'They alone give life to my dresses, I cannot think of one without the other.' He had his favourites—there was wayward Tania whom he had known since she was sixteen when they had both worked for designer Lucien Lelong, 'Of all the mannequins I have known, Tania is one of the most naturally and extraordinarily gifted for the job . . . in only a few days all the tricks of the trade were familiar to her, and from the very first showing she had a way of modelling that was all her own.'

Left: Victoire, the girl with the Left Bank look who became first Dior's and then Yves Saint Laurent's favourite model. When she retired from modelling she opened her own boutique in Paris.
Right: Sumurun dressed for a fashion show at Olympia in 1923, the year Tutankhamun's tomb was discovered. Molyneux's Pharaoh-inspired costume suited Sumurun's dark and mysterious looks to perfection.

He loved the model France for her height, her slenderness and her pale beauty. 'She was the greatest mannequin I ever had—typically Parisienne and always a success, the audience would applaud her wildly.' He admired poor unlucky Lucky who tried so hard and died too young. 'Lucky did not become a model because she was pretty,' Dior said, 'she became pretty because she wished to be a model.' He was referring to the fact that she had undergone several facial plastic surgery operations. 'Every entrance she makes is preceded for her by intense concentration. She thinks and translates the intentions of the dress. She does not wear it, she acts it.'

He said that Alla, the extraordinary arrogant-looking Oriental, had more 'presence' than any other girl. 'There is a sort of perversity about showing dresses destined for Western women on an Asian beauty. But Alla is half-Russian and if her face has all the mysteries of the Orient, her body is perfectly European. I know that a woman who chooses one of her models will not be disappointed.'

He hired the petite dark Victoire the very day before the showing of a new collection, and no one could understand why. His colleagues protested that she was too small and didn't know how to walk, but Dior wanted her. He thought she was different: 'She had a little Left Bank look that pleased me. I promised to make her one or two dresses and during the fittings I realized more and more that she could be a star.' But Victoire was not a success—some thought her 'little Left Bank look' a downright insult to his rich, and definitely Right Bank, clientele. But Dior held firm, and Victoire was allowed to show the collection again a season later. This time the audience were enthusiastic and called her 'the very spirit of youth'. 'They said I had changed her,' said Dior, 'but it was they that had changed.'

When Dior died in 1958, the young Yves Saint Laurent inherited his throne and Victoire became his favourite mannequin. Her Left Bank look was just right for his youthful designs. Saint Laurent's first collection for the house of Dior was successful but his next two were considered far too young and altogether unsuitable for this grand house. Whether by accident or design, Saint Laurent was suddenly called up for his national service in the French army. He had a nervous breakdown and was more or less forgotten by everyone except Victoire. She doggedly continued to believe in him throughout the trying time of his collapse, recovery and attempts to find finance to enable him to open his own business. Victoire even persuaded her dressmaker mother to come up from the country to run Saint Laurent's work room. And when eventually he did show his own collection in 1962, it was Victoire who stepped out first to open the show. She wore what became an immensely popular outfit, a sailor jacket with white bell-bottom trousers. Saint Laurent was launched.

The designer Jacques Fath prided himself on having a good-looking stable of girls rivalled only by that of Dior. In the early fifties the highest paid mannequin in Paris was Fath's Bettina,

Coco Chanel with the American beauty Suzy Parker, who modelled Chanel's clothes in the late fifties and became her favourite.

who later became famous as Prince Aly Khan's last love. She had come to him as Simone Bodin, the daughter of a French railway worker. She was a raw-boned, freckly, red-headed country bumpkin, and Fath groomed her into a beauty and changed her name. It was in Fath's salon that the Prince first caught sight of Bettina when he came to see a collection with Rita Hayworth. But it was not until 1955 that Bettina retired from modelling to live with him, a liaison that ended tragically after his death in a car crash in 1960. In the meantime her beauty, charm and flair for clothes had made Bettina a popular cover girl in France, as well as Fath's star.

When Bettina left him to work for Givenchy, Fath's inspiration became Sophie Malga, a ravishing girl known as 'the incomparable Sophie' who later married Anatole Litvak, the film producer.

Post-war Paris was dominated by men designers until 1954 when Coco Chanel re-opened her business. The pundits predicted that her comeback after fifteen years would be disastrous, but within a year she had the fashion world at her feet again. It was not just her clothes that were more relaxed than everyone else's, but also the girls who modelled them. Chanel's mannequins were well-bred girls who came from some of the best families in Europe. 'They're bored,' said Chanel acidly. 'Their mothers and grandmothers had a different occupation: love. The men in their circles didn't work. Those men were always available for love. But what man today could indulge in such absorbing passions? So these girls 'phone one another to exchange stupidities: "Shall we go to work for Chanel? Some of the crowd will be there, and besides there are the clothes."' She described how the girls used to lie in wait for her old suits— 'The more worn the suits are, the more pleased the girls seem to be to get them.'

In Chanel's scented salon there was none of the theatrical spinning and whirling and knocking-over of ashtrays or notebooks. Chanel trained her models to walk as she did, with hips forward, hands in pockets—very easy, very feminine. Somehow she succeeded in making them all look like carbon copies of herself when younger. They wore her clothes and accessories exactly the way she did herself, and they were made to adopt Chanel's hairstyles, and even follow the way she made up with arched brows and rouged cheeks. She managed to create self-portraits out of the most unlikely looking women—the glorious redhead Suzy Parker, for instance, who in the late fifties became Chanel's favourite, the archetypal Chanel girl. Marie-Helene Arnaud was another successful photographic

Left: Sophie Malga was an exquisite, fine-featured girl who became Jacques Fath's top model and inspiration. *Right*: One of Chanel's favourite models was Marie-Hélène Arnaud, who resembled Chanel herself when young. For a time it was rumoured that Marie-Hélène would take over the business.

model who went to work for Chanel in the fifties and, until they quarrelled, she was tipped to one day take over the business. 'They were destroying her when I began to take an interest in her,' said Chanel; 'magazines use you and spit you out. So I was a good angel for her.' Marie-Helene with her dark fringe and lively face was the girl most like Mademoiselle, and she looked marvellous in her clothes, but her career in the Rue Cambon ended, it is said, because she got too grand and came to think of herself as indispensible. Chanel eventually became rather bitter about her models: 'They are beautiful, that's why they can get these jobs. If they were intelligent they'd give them up. All they think of is money. They don't care a single damn about you. They come here looking like housemaids on a day off and they leave looking like scrubwomen.'

Occasionally the model who is the designer's inspiration can be everyone else's pain in the neck. In the early sixties Pierre Cardin had as his star a tiny, doll-like Japanese model called Hiroko. He made all his best clothes on her, so it followed that hers were the numbers all the magazines and papers wanted to photograph. I was then working for the *Sunday Times* and we had booked our own model on whom we intended to photo-graph all the Paris clothes. I can still remember how desperate

Above: Pupils hard at work learning social etiquette in the thirties with teacher Sylvia Gollidge (alias Lucie Clayton) standing second from the left. *Right:* Hiroko, the doll-like Japanese model, was Pierre Cardin's favourite in the mid-sixties. She was so tiny that no other model girl could fit into her clothes.

124

we were on discovering that none of the Cardin clothes we had chosen had a hope of fitting her. At three o'clock in the morning I had to make my weary way to Montmartre where Hiroko lived and persuade her to get out of bed, make up her face and come back with me to the studio to wear the clothes which, like Cinderella's glass slipper, only fitted her frail figure.

In 1964 it was my turn to witness a revolution in fashion and fashion showing. Until that year, guests at a dress show in Paris always sat on spindly gilt chairs in *salons* which were usually decorated in the rather grand style of one of the Kings Louis. There was never any background music, or indeed noise of any sort—only the voice of the *vendeuses* calling out the numbers of the garments. In January 1964, the journalists filing into the

Tall, suntanned, lean and leggy, the star at Courrèges was Monique, photographed (twice) below in 1964, wearing the new shockingly short hem length.

Courrèges *salon* in Paris were astonished to find themselves in a stark modern room with white vinyl walls and white boxes to sit on. Loud beat music was playing and when the show started, giant girls with close-cropped hair, freckles, suntans and wide, white grins came pounding out wearing skirts inches above the knees and flat white boots. Courrèges was launching his 'space-age' clothes and he was shrewd enough to know that it would be useless to show such revolutionary ideas unless you did it on a new kind of girl in a new kind of *salon*.

Back in England Mary Quant had also understood this, and a large part of her success in the late fifties was due to the way in which she presented her clothes and the girls she chose as models. 'I want girls who exaggerate the realness of themselves, not their haughty unrealness like the couture models do.' Quant's clothes were first shown in, of all places, the old-fashioned Palace Hotel in St Moritz. She had been invited to bring over some garments as part of an all-British fashion promotion. As all the other, far grander outfits were being unpacked she saw with increasing gloom that her simple styles would be lost among them. Something had to be done. She insisted that her own small group of clothes be shown to hot jazz music, and she quickly put her mannequins through some unconventional paces. The Quant models opened the show in the staid ballroom of the Palace. They kicked up their legs, they danced, they ran, they jumped, they took up crazy poses. In Quant's words, 'The whole atmosphere was electrified. Nobody in the audience had seen this sort of thing before.'

She repeated the idea for her very first press show in London, using a wind machine to blow the models' skirts to create an even greater swirling sense of speed and movement, and with jazz music specially taped in advance. 'We showed forty garments in fifteen minutes and every single minute was packed with incident. The girls just threw themselves into the spirit of the whole thing and acted like mad.' Girls wearing sporty clothes were accessoried with shotguns and dead pheasants from Harrods across the road. When they swung these about blood spattered over the audience. Quant's was christened 'the whackiest show ever'.

Throughout the Swinging Sixties the crazy fashion show was the thing. The models behaved more and more dottily, the music blared louder and louder, the *venues* grew more and more eccentric and uncomfortable, and by the end of the decade one was longing for the boring old days of gilt chairs and no head-ache.

When clothes sobered up in the seventies, so inevitably did fashion shows and became almost as respectable as they had been in the fifties. But there is a difference. A designer may well have a theme for his collection, but in these days of anarchy in fashion, the audience certainly doesn't. Now, one can while away idle moments at shows rapt in the astonishing clothes of one's colleagues, who may be dressed in anything from checked travelling rugs to sweaters with crotch-high boots, to gardening aprons and slippers.

9 That Special Face

I have worked with model girls who have been 'discovered' on trains, in schoolrooms, behind the counters in boutiques, at the hairdressers, or have simply been picked up in the street. Fashion photography devours them insatiably and the search is ever on for a new face. I remember walking down the Kings Road in Chelsea with a photographer who couldn't bear to let a pretty girl slip through his fingers. He stopped a lovely looking creature and told her, 'You could be a *great* model'. She answered coldly in a thick foreign accent, 'I am'. We retired, crushed.

It is difficult to describe the quality in a girl that brings a picture to life and makes other women want to look like her or to buy the clothes she is wearing. You can ring round the model agencies and ask them to send you all the blondes on their books with brown eyes and big mouths, the girls will file in clutching their portfolios and not one of them need have what you are looking for. When bathing suits with exaggeratedly high-cut legs became fashionable in the summer of 1976 and I needed to photograph one, I called in all the tall, dark, strong-featured girls I could find, but my photographer Norman Eales picked out the only short, sweet-looking girl in the group. Until I saw the prints of that swimsuit picture I thought Eales was wrong, but he had seen something in this girl that was perfect for the picture he had in mind.

It goes without saying that a model must have a face that fits the fashions of the moment. The mature and sophisticated women of the fifties died the death in the sixties, when youth was the thing (try imagining Barbara Goalen in a mini-skirt), just as the pretty girls-next-door of the sixties have had to yield to much harder, stronger-looking beauties in the seventies, simply because the complex clothes of this decade need tough faces to carry them off. It helps if a girl is intelligent, but it isn't vital. David Bailey once worked with a top girl who was so slow on the uptake that she didn't realize he'd gone for lunch during the photo session. He found her two hours later still valiantly holding the complicated pose he'd left her in at the end of the morning.

When a session goes right, in Jean Shrimpton's words, 'suddenly it all happens. You feel the mood of the clothes, you feel irresistably attractive, you give the whole essence of yourself to the camera.' John French, the great British photographer of the fifties, experienced 'girls with whom you can take hundreds of shots but the session becomes dead. Then there are girls whose alchemy is right. Their personality suddenly

Right: Simone d'Aillencourt, the ultra-sophisticated French model, at the height of her career. *Overleaf:* Marie Helvin, a star of the seventies, whose oriental face and beautiful body have made her the perfect model for the exotic fashions—and fashion pictures—of this decade.

bubbles, they react and make that fantastic rapport between the photographer and the model which makes for a lively and exciting picture. They may be in the wrong age group, they may know the dress exposes their worst feature, but they get in front of the camera and the magic starts. It is almost impossible to take a bad picture of them, however dowdy their clothes.' Tania Mallett, a top sixties model, said that being photographed by the great Richard Avedon was like 'having your soul sucked out through your eye sockets'. Avedon confesses 'I am always a little in love with my girls'.

When a session goes well and the man behind the camera and the girl in front of it are locked into an intense exchange of feeling, a fashion editor in the studio can feel like an intruder. The photographer coaxes, bullies and flatters with an endless stream of chat: 'Divine, divine . . . hold it . . . hold it . . . HOLD IT . . . wet your lips . . . fantastic, marvellous . . . don't move . . . say Friday . . . say Thursday . . . great . . . great . . . lick your lips again . . . that's GREAT, doll . . . you're marvellous baby.' Inevitably some of the great photographer/model combinations have been husbands and wives or lovers. Irving Penn married the celebrated model Lisa Fonssagrives; the eccentric Norman Parkinson, whose sessions have been described as circus sideshows, worked with his wife, Wenda; in Paris Peter Knapp and Nicole de la Margé created magical pictures during the time they lived together; and the work of Jean Shrimpton and David Bailey as a team during their three-and-a-half year liaison made them both world famous. When that came to an end you could tell who was Bailey's current love by flipping through *Vogue* and picking out his best photographs.

Eileen Ford, known as 'The Godmother' in the American fashion business, has built up the most prestigous model agency in the world. She started it in 1948 when she was pregnant and short of money. Nowadays her constant search for new faces lures her from New York to Europe about four times a year, on what can literally be called girl-hunts. 'I am after the star. The sixteen-year-old whose single untrained glance lets editors, photographers and customers know that whatever it is they've been looking for, they've found.' When and if she finds her, Ms Ford will take the girl to America, invite her to stay, feed her, train her, polish her, groom her and cherish her like a daughter. A star can earn a million dollars in the course of her career and naturally Ms Ford's agency get their commission: among others Eileen Ford nurtured the modelling careers of Candice Bergen, Elsa Martinelli, and Ali McGraw.

Talent-spotting for special faces has been happening since fashion photography took off in the early twenties. One of Britain's first fashion photographers was Shaw Wildman: 'I was always on the lookout. Accosting attractive young females in restaurants or in the streets was an occupational hazard. The more fashionable or exclusive the restaurant or street, the easier it was to land the catch. Searching among thousands of holiday-makers on Blackpool beach in the hope of finding a suitable

133

subject was a total waste of time. I did see one or two I thought possible, but they and their parents were deeply suspicious—they were sure there must be a catch in it.' He scanned theatrical agencies with some success. He found one Micky Hood, for instance, among the stage and film extras gathered hopefully in an office in Wardour Street, in Soho. 'They were treated with scant respect. From time to time the waiting-room pigeon hole would shoot up and a loud voice bellow, "CLEAR OUT, CLEAR OUT, ALL OF YOU". But Micky Hood was in luck that day. I booked her on the spot.' Ms Hood had a long and successful career as a model, mostly in advertising shots, and she was the first of the Kodak cardboard cut-out girls that used to stand outside chemist shops.

Model agencies helped a little when they opened up at the end of the twenties and in the thirties, though in their early days these concentrated on running charm courses for gauche young girls, or had only show models on their books. A refined magazine editor told me once how shocked she had been when agencies became more orientated towards photography and spoke openly about girls' measurements, 'as though they were prize cattle'.

Until the Second World War brought democracy into the clothing business, the influential fashion pictures were nearly always of couture garments, elegant, and of course expensive. These would often be photographed on society beauties who were cajoled into doing it for prestige, or on actresses who needed publicity. It helped in those days, I am told, if the models came from good backgrounds. Only a girl accustomed to wearing expensive clothes, jewellery, hats and gloves had the necessary poise to cope in front of the camera. Since the most desirable couture clothes were still made in Paris, that was the city to which fashion photographers and aspiring model girls gravitated.

Less effort went into preparing the girls for the pictures, than into perfecting the backgrounds. Photographers scoured around for witty and appropriate props and would paint the most elaborate scenery for their pictures. Cecil Beaton was a past master at this. He used mirrors to give infinite reflections, paper hoops through which his subjects burst like circus dogs, fake snow, painted landscapes, plaster busts and miles of tulle. (When he was only a young boy, still experimenting with ideas, he made his sister pose with her head under one of those glass domes the Victorians put over dried flower arrangements. Every time she breathed the glass became clouded. Beaton bullied her to hold her breath until she nearly asphyxiated.) Nowadays, however, so many fashion pictures are taken for newspapers in which backgrounds do not reproduce clearly that photographers tend to concentrate more on the girl herself. Hairdressers and make-up artists are brought into the studio to groom her, and it may sometimes take hours of concentrated

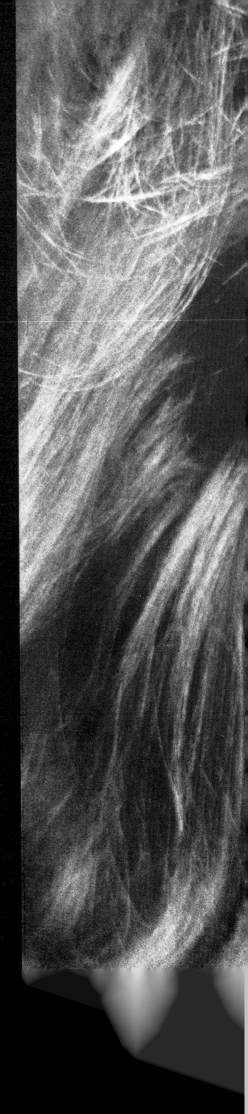

Photographic models have a curious kind of fame. They may have their faces plastered over ten-foot-high hoardings, but nobody really knows *who* they are. Only the handful who reach the very top acquire a name, a personality and a private life that inevitably gets into the gossip columns. Even then there is a catch, because that kind of publicity can be the kiss of death for a model—it makes *her* more important than the clothes she is supposed to be selling. She can't be used for ordinary fashion features, and if her face becomes too familiar she won't be used at all.

The nameless girls whose careers endure for years are the chameleons who lose their own identities in whatever the fashion of the moment happens to be. But the girls who become household names, the Barbara Goalens and Jean Shrimptons, have a look that is all their own: a look that is exactly right for its time and is the very essence of how women want to be— just at that moment.

There were stars among the models as early as in the late twenties. Lee Miller was one of the first and the loveliest faces to acquire a name. She was an American who stopped in Paris *en route* to a finishing school in the South of France, and never got any further. 'I thought, "Baby I'm home", and I stayed on.' Her father broadmindedly gave her the money that was to have paid her school fees and she got a job working backstage in the theatre. 'I was nineteen, but I wasn't scared. I loved everything. It was 1925—a terrific time, I felt everything opening up in front of me.' Lee Miller went back to the States after a year and met the photographer Steichen who was then working for *Vogue*—and he asked her to pose for him. 'I really was terribly, terribly pretty. I looked like an angel, but I was a fiend inside.' In 1927 she returned to Paris and became a model, working mainly with George Hoyningen-Huene, the frightening German Baron who would look scornfully at the nervous models waiting for him and say, 'Is this what you expect me to photograph?' After a couple of years, the lovely Miss Miller decided she'd had enough and that it would be more satisfying to be on the other side of the camera. She made up her mind to learn the trade by apprenticing herself to the most exciting photographer of the day, Man Ray.

When she presented herself at his studio, to her disappointment the concierge explained that Monsieur had just left for Biarritz. Miss Miller went to a nearby café to console herself with a drink. She was sitting gloomily in the bar when suddenly Man Ray appeared. 'He kind of rose up through the floor at the top of a circular staircase. He looked like a bull, with an extraordinary torso and very dark eyebrows and dark hair. I told him boldly that I was his new student. He said he didn't take students and anyway he was leaving Paris for his holiday. I said I know, I'm going with you—and I did. We lived together for three years. I was known as Madame Man Ray, because that's how they do things in France.' Miss Miller learnt her photography and Man Ray in turn photographed her. They eventu-

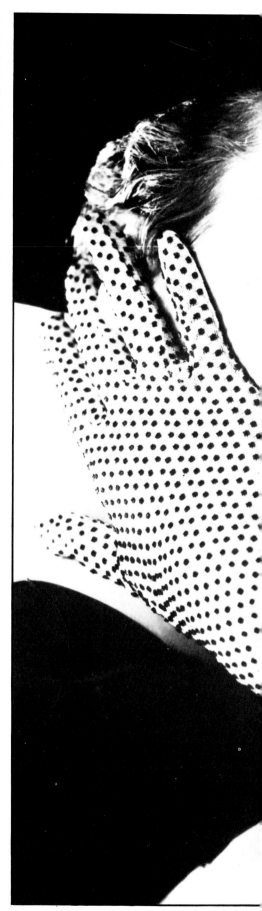

ally quarrelled over an Egyptian with whom Lee Miller had fallen in love and later married.

During the Second World War, Lee Miller made her name as a war photographer, and after it she married the art historian and collector, Sir Roland Penrose. In 1960 she retired from photography, and has not taken a picture since. 'You can't be an amateur,' she says, 'when you have been a professional.'

Soon after Lee Miller had concluded her modelling career, Toto Koopman embarked on hers. Where Lee Miller's had been a fresh-faced, blonde beauty, Toto Koopman's was dark and secret with a hint of the East. She had Javanese and Chinese blood inherited on her mother's side of the family who were Dutch from the East Indies. She had been born in Java, and schooled in Holland and England. But at the end of the 1920s she was living in Paris and working as a mannequin, first for Chanel, and later for Marcel Rochas—'I was just about getting fed up with show modelling—it was awfully tiring—when by sheer chance I met a German girl who was posing for Hoyningen-Huene. She took me to meet him and he said he'd try a picture with me. It seemed to be a success and after that I worked with him all the time: he didn't like his models to be used by other photographers.' Ms Koopman was one of Hoyningen-Huene's favourites from 1930 onwards, but by 1933 she was a little bored with Paris. Alexander Korda, the film director, was auditioning girls for his picture *The Love Life of Don Juan*, so Toto Koopman came to England and landed a part, which she soon lost when she failed to report for work one morning. They did, however, use her picture for the film publicity. In London she fell in love with Lord Beaverbrook's son, Max Aitken, and they lived together for some time—very daring in those days. She survived a frightful war, imprisoned in Ravensbruk concentration camp, and afterwards came back to live in London.

By the mid-thirties the photographer of the day was Horst who had been Hoyningen-Huene's friend and assistant and now worked for *Vogue* himself. The models Horst has worked with and made famous are many, but he says that his favourites at that time were undoubtedly the Swedish beauty Lisa Fonssagrives, who was renowned for her superb body and lovely face, and Lude, a temperamental Russian girl living in Paris who had unsuccessful plastic surgery done on her breasts and couldn't wear any dress cut too low because her nipples pointed upwards. In Paris, Horst also liked to work with Agneta Fischer, a German girl, and in America his preferred models were Helen Bennett and Muriel Maxwell. All these he judged to have the right look for the right time, but he had no need to tread the streets in search of these girls because they simply turned up on his doorstep.

Madame Muthe, a refugee from Nazi Germany, arrived unannounced like this in the *Vogue* office in Paris not long before the outbreak of war. She waited holding her baby in her arms, and together they made such a lovely sight that the

Previous page: Barbara Goalen was 33 years old when this picture was taken in 1953. Aloof and worldly-wise, hers was the face of the decade.

Lee Miller (photographed below in 1932) was perhaps the best known of the early photographic models. She decided to become a photographer, and apprenticed herself to Man Ray who took the picture of her (*right*) in 1931. The lighting he used was from her sunray lamp.

138

Editor of *Vogue* rushed to the fashion office saying, 'Come quickly and see the Virgin Mary and the Infant Jesus.' From then, Muthe enjoyed a brief moment of fame, but it was not to last: during the occupation of Paris she was killed by the Gestapo because she fell in love with a German captain, when she was supposed to be reserved solely for the entertainment of German high generals.

But Paris, in that last summer before the outbreak of war in September 1939, was gayer and more frivolous than ever before—it was to be the last fling for the snobbish, extravagant world of high society and high fashion. The War was the great leveller, and all women were equal when it came to rationing, utility and clothing coupons. Fashion journalists in Britain told their readers how to make do and mend, how to sew an evening skirt out of blackout material or transform one simple jumper into several—'wear a necklace one day, none the next, and clips the day after. It will look different again if you wear it with rolled up sleeves the way the American girls are doing.' In America the L 85 restrictions ensured that clothes were more or less straight up and down so that as little cloth as possible was used. *Vogue* took to photographing their smart socialites at war work. The 1930s high fashion model had no place in this world of austerity and a new kind of girl had to be found to model the utility frocks, someone ordinary, cheerful, smiling through. Jane Webb, *Picture Post*'s most popular cover girl was a typical war-time ideal.

Fashion, however, stood still until 1947 when Christian Dior opened his new couture house in Paris with a collection of the prettiest clothes that had been seen for eight years. His dresses took up metres and metres of cloth in their long swinging skirts; dainty high-heeled shoes, adorable hand-span waists and gentle sloping shoulders gave women back their femininity. In spite of critics who bemoaned the folly of such extravagance, women starved of such things fell on Dior's New Look and devoured it whole. The ready-to-wear industry was now in full swing and able to knock out copies for everyone to wear.

The New Look entirely changed the way women dressed. An Irving Penn photograph of the twelve top models in New York taken the same year shows how quickly it was adopted. Every one of them has eyebrows plucked into haughty arches, their hair glossy and groomed, and swept back into chignons. Their ages you would guess as in the mid-thirties and they all look like the kind of women who use long black cigarette holders and blow smoke into your face.

Simone d'Aillencourt (who was the very first French photographic model to make the big time) had this arrogant, worldly air to perfection, complete with a saucy black beauty spot on her chin. Simone, though her appearance was ultra-*Parisienne*, became a model in London. She actually only came to England to improve her languages, but so many people asked her if she was a fashion model that she decided she should train at Lucie Clayton. In those days the model girl was responsible for her

Lauren Hutton, who in 1973 became the most highly paid model in history.

Left: Margaux Hemingway beat Lauren Hutton's record as the most highly paid model when she signed a one million dollar contract to promote a new perfume, Babe, in 1976. *Right:* Toto Koopman, a well-known model from 1930–33. 'She was like an exquisite gazelle.' *Below:* Helen Bennett, an American model who was one of photographer Horst's favourites.

own hair, make-up and accessories. Simone quickly gained a reputation for being able to cope better than anyone. 'I don't think I am pretty or beautiful, but I do love fashion and I could transform myself very quickly to suit whatever I was wearing.' She was famed throughout the fashion business for her magician-like ability to change her hair. She worked with switches, falls and wigs, changing them as the situation demanded. Simone now runs her own model agency in Paris.

In the fifties it was the English who blossomed as models. That decade produced some stunning beauties and their names were world-famous. When Barbara Goalen married in 1953, hundreds of rubber-neckers turned up at Caxton Hall to see their heroine, and newspapers reported every tiny detail of her trousseau. This was an inconceivable kind of fame for a mere model to achieve, and it came about because for the first time high-fashion pictures were appearing in mass circulation news-papers and not just in the glossies like *Vogue* and *Harper's*. This small revolution we owe largely to the photographer John French. French had once worked for a firm of engravers and was experienced in the problems of reproducing photographs in newsprint, problems which led to fashion editors using mostly

Above: The blonde beauty Muthe poses in a Balenciaga dress in Helena Rubinstein's fabulous apartment in Paris. *Left:* Muriel Maxwell, another Horst favourite.

Right: One of the prettiest models in the fifties was Enid Munnick, who came to London from South Africa. Her daughter, Ingrid Boulting, followed in her footsteps.

Below: During the War the high fashion model had no place, and newspapers chose more ordinary, cheerful-looking girls to pose in utility clothes. Jane Webb was *Picture Post*'s most popular cover girl.

sketches to illustrate the clothes they picked. French developed a system of lighting his photographs that made them so clear and so sharp that they still looked good on the inky pages of, for instance, the *Daily Express*.

One of his models was Jean Dawnay. She described his lighting in her book *Model Girl*: 'I was standing on white paper and there was more behind me and in front. I was in a sort of white box. . . . None of the big studio lights were directed on to me; instead they were aimed at the white paper, so I stood in reflected light.'

John French's model girls always looked perfect: his re-touchers whisked off all creases, wrinkles and blemishes. There is an old snapshot of John French aged about seven on holiday, which shows him pulling at his little sister's bathing cap with exactly the same expression on his face as I noticed years later when I used to watch him twitching at the models' clothes to get them looking right, and choosing their accessories; these were usually white gloves and pearls from the vast horde that he kept in the studio. His star was Barbara Goalen. Her measurements were $33\frac{1}{2}$–21–$33\frac{1}{2}$, which made her a perfect shape for the pencil-slim skirts and nipped-in jackets of the fifties. She had exquisitely small hands and feet, and a nose that had been trimmed by plastic surgery. The newspapers called her 'Queen of the Mannequins', 'Glittering Goalen', 'The Girl with the Mink and Diamond look'. A popular version of her story is that she was found by an agent sitting on a suitcase at Basingstoke station with two children clinging to her bosom and tears pouring down her face. He discovered she was recently widowed took pity on her and sent her to see John French. . . . The truth is a little less dramatic. Her husband, it is true, was an airline pilot and had been killed in 1947, and she did have two children and needed work. But it was she who felt that her figure entitled her to have a crack at modelling. She got herself an introduction to a couturier, worked for him as a show model and then went freelance. 'I started that business of trailing all the fabulous furs around on the floor when I was doing shows. Before I came into it models used to hold them reverently off the ground. I just used to sling 'em around as though they were made of sacking.'

Barbara Goalen made everything she wore look like a million dollars, but in fact most of the clothes she modelled were off-the-peg. She and John French liked to cook up ingenious fashion ideas that could be copied by *Daily Express* readers—one popular story was on the different ways a girl could look good in a man's shirt.

Fiona Campbell Walter was an equally legendary beauty. She had red hair and green eyes—one enthusiastic reporter compared her with Helen of Troy. Her lovely face inspired fan mail from across the world. She once had a letter from a group of miners in Cuba, and another from two pilgrims en route to Mecca: hardly *Vogue* readers, one would have thought.

Fiona Campbell Walter's father was an admiral, and she came into modelling when she was eighteen simply by spending £25 on a Lucie Clayton course. In 1956 she retired and married the wealthy Baron von Thyssen but they divorced in 1965. Her name next appeared in the headlines linked with Alexander Onassis, many years her junior. His father Aristotle did not approve and is supposed to have said before his son's coming-of-age, 'Alexander can have anything he wants for his birthday. Anything but Fiona.'

The American agent Eileen Ford still thinks that Ann Gunning was one of the loveliest girls she has ever had on her books. Ms Gunning Parker (her real name) had jet black hair, a pale face and a 'withdrawn, Garbo-like quality'. She was descended from the famous Gunning sisters who took Irish society by storm in the eighteenth century. (Maria Gunning died of poisoning from the white lead with which she painted her face.) In 1961 Anne Gunning married politician Anthony Nutting, and the newspapers observed that 'She is the only candidate's wife to have been a cover-girl on *Life* magazine'.

John French preferred his models to look like real people; he liked to bring out their awareness, intelligence and personality, and that is why he liked working with beautiful blonde Susan Abraham. 'She starts off with beauty of a touchingly simple

Right: Barbara Goalen in an early fifties fashion feature on the many ways a girl could look good in a man's shirt. She stopped modelling in 1954, but 23 years later she consented to pose for the picture on the far right.

kind,' he once said. 'Her loosely brushed hair doesn't look as if a hairdresser had been torturing it, her skin is shining with health, her mouth is lipsticked but not "improved" into a grotesque shape.'

Working with John French could be a tremendous boost for a model. He had a way of transforming a pretty girl into a luminous beauty, and if he chose to work with her he could establish her career. Fully aware of this, the first time Marla Scarafia, a young Italian, came to his studio she crushed her finger in the door of her taxi, but she was so scared he might turn her away if he knew she was fainting with pain that she said nothing. She became a favourite French model and later a film actress. In the same way he groomed Paulene Stone, a model whose career went on to span more than twenty years since she started by winning a modelling competition run by *Womans Own*.

All these girls were the darlings of the newspapers. They were the last society girls in a world that was about to be blown apart by the pop explosion that was Swinging London. John French's girls still lived in places like Belgravia (even if it was just a flat), they wore hats and gloves and pearls and dressed as elegantly off the set as on. They spent their nights foxtrotting in smart clubs like The Four Hundred, escorted by wealthy upper-class men whom they often married. 'Every schoolgirl reads of the parties, the peers and the presents that are so much part of the glittering Goalen story.' The dawning of the sixties meant goodbye to all that forever.

Jean Shrimpton is always described as waif-like, but I think she was more like the heroine of a horsey book for teenage girls. Tall, gangling, tomboyish with a wide smiley mouth and untidy brown hair, she had been brought up on a farm and she was crazy about dogs and horses. She once said that she was more thrilled with the first rosette she won at a gymkhana than with her first cover picture for *Vogue*. She went to a convent, was a keen hockey player and got her O levels in eight subjects. Then, in 1959 when she was seventeen, she came to London— 'as green as spring salad'—to do a secretarial course. A couple of times during that first year in London people approached her suggesting that she should try modelling, so with her parents' blessing she went to the Lucie Clayton modelling school. In class she found herself sitting next to a young blonde called Celia Hammond, and the very first press picture of either of these girls was taken by the *Evening News*. It shows them, grinning and gauche, after the Lucie Clayton passing out

Fiona Campbell Walter (*right*) with her red hair and green eyes was a legendary fifties beauty. On the far right she is pictured at 18, before she completed a modelling course.

Above: Susan Abraham 'starts with beauty of a touchingly simple kind', said the photographer John French.

Below: Ann Gunning is considered by her one-time agent Eileen Ford to have been one of the loveliest girls she has ever had on her books.

parade. That was in 1960, and Jean plodded round the photographers' studios. She found work and Norman Eales even predicted to the *Evening Standard* that hers would be the face of 1961. But it was not until she worked with David Bailey that her star (and his) rose so spectacularly: 'I know how lucky I was to arrive on the scene just at that time. The unladylike, tomboy, off-beat fashions came in just as I started and were responsible in some way for my success.' Youth was the thing in the early sixties and soon every girl wanted to look like Jean with her tousled mane of hair, pale lips, enormous eyes and long legs. By 1964 she was famous enough to write her memoirs, and even the other top models of the time, Tania Mallett and Celia Hammond, and later Sue Murray, projected something of *her* look.

During my early days as a fashion writer at the beginning of the sixties I often worked with Shrimpton and Bailey. There was none of the big studio efficiency, no assistants, props or pinnings, no careful retouching, but it was fun. The worst session we did was when we were sent for the first time to do the Paris collections for the *Sunday Times Magazine*. There was a jinx on the trip. Both Bailey's cameras broke and we had to borrow an unfamiliar make from a photographer friend. Then I couldn't resist trying on one of the dresses we had borrowed from a couture house to photograph. I climbed on to my bed in the hotel to get a better view of myself in the mirror, and of course I fell and put my foot through the hem and tore yards and yards of the pleated green chiffon. I sat up half the night cobbling it together with darning thread. At first light we arrived in the gardens of the Palace of Versailles for the session. It was a bitterly cold January morning and all the clothes were summer frocks. There was nowhere to change so Jean had to strip off behind a neatly clipped hedge. Bailey shouted, Jean cried and I was torn between worrying whether we'd ever warm Jean up again and whether her purple goosepimples would show in the pictures.

In 1965, a fibre company sponsored Jean on a publicity trip to Australia. They got more than they bargained for in the way of newspaper coverage: Jean appeared at Melbourne races in an above-the-knee skirt (hardly shocking by our later standards) and without hat or gloves. The Australian papers screamed with 'Who-Does-She-Think-She-Is?' fury. But it only added to her fame. Towards the end of the sixties she went to work in America, and then retired from modelling altogether. Now she lives quietly in the West Country of England and can only be lured away to work on very special jobs with photographer friends like Bailey or Richard Avedon.

Jean Shrimpton was the blueprint for beauty in the first half of the sixties, but in 1966 a schoolgirl called Lesley Hornby from the London suburb of Neasden had the kind of overnight success that every kid dreams of. Twiggy, as she was known, was only sixteen, but her boyfriend, Justin de Villeneuve, was a budding man of the world. He thought she might make a model so together they went to see *Queen* magazine (where

John French was expert at grooming model girls. Marla Scarafia came to him as a pretty but unexciting girl (above right) and he transformed her into the dazzling beauty on the left.

they got the brush off) and *Woman's Mirror* who sent Twiggy to the hairdresser Leonard to have something done about her straggly locks. Leonard clipped her head short and had some photographs done of her which were spotted in his salon by Deirdre McSharry, fashion editor of the *Daily Express*. She called Twiggy and Justin to the paper. A whole page of the *Express* headlined THIS IS THE FACE OF '66 was devoted to Twiggy—'the cockney kid with the face to launch a thousand shapes—and she's only sixteen. Three weeks ago she left school, now she is making £100 a week.' 'In fact,' says Twiggy, 'I hadn't made any money at all.'

She soon did. It was Twiggy that the youngsters suddenly wanted to look like. Twiggy, with her ungainly stance, her tiny skirt, her skimpy sweaters, her long legs (often carefully posed to look knock-kneed). She was the first unisex model—'*Garçon ou fille?*' asked *Paris Match* when they put her on their cover. Twiggy became a craze: car stickers said FORGET OXFAM FEED TWIGGY, there were Twiggy clothes, Twiggy eyelashes, Twiggy dummies in shop windows and in Madame Tussaud's. Twiggy was taken to Paris to comment on the collections, and her ingenuous remarks—'most of Balmain's clothes were a bit of a giggle'—were quoted by reporters who took care to reproduce her cockney accent in print. When Twiggy and Justin went to New York to launch Twiggy dresses they had to employ body-

Right: Paulene Stone, soon after winning a modelling competition run by *Woman's Own* some twenty years ago. *Far right:* Jean Shrimpton (on the right) and Celia Hammond went to the same modelling school, Lucie Clayton's. This picture of the two girls, both as yet unknown, was taken by a newspaper photographer the day they left.

guards to save them from the curiosity of the crowds who pressed round them.

Some looked on her as a kind of manufactured model, a deliberately conceived publicity stunt, and they predicted only a flash-in-the-pan success. But Twiggy denies this, 'The look I wore then wasn't carefully worked out or calculated. It was just the way Justin and I liked me to look. He gave me the idea for drawing eyelashes under my eyes which he copied from a doll he had.' And Justin says, 'I didn't do anything deliberately for the sake of a certain image. Everyone assumed we were a put-on but it wasn't an act at all.'

Twiggy survived her teenage years and her teenage image, and towards the end of the sixties she changed her dolly look for a more nostalgic and feminine one. 'I'm not a modern girl at all. My head's completely in the past. I've always been into the thirties thing. I really love that period. I started wanting to look like my heroine Greta Garbo.' In 1971 Twiggy appeared in her first movie *The Boyfriend*, singing and dancing, and getting good reviews. She succeeded in changing not only her look but her career as well, a difficult switch for such a familiar face.

Throughout the sixties, fashions came and went with the speed of a camera shutter. Unless you were a personality (like Shrimpton or Twiggy) the only way a model could survive for long was to adapt her appearance to every change. Grace Coddington was so good at this, so expert at putting together the various looks, that it was natural for her to become a *Vogue* fashion editor in the end. Grace won a *Vogue* model contest in 1959 when she was eighteen and working as a part-time waitress in London. 'We think she'll do more modelling than

waiting,' was *Vogue*'s coy comment. In those early days she looked like a shy young debutante, but soon she ran the gamut of the many and varied fashions of the sixties. Grace always adopted the latest make-up and hairstyles, she never had a misplaced scarf, belt or bag. She was a perfect clothes-horse, the kind of model girl that you can't easily identify.

By 1968 all the rules in fashion had been broken. Skirts had got shorter than anyone would have thought possible, sunglasses bigger, colours brighter, furs wilder, boots kinkier. And in fashion photography most of the gimmicks had been used up. We had had girls suspended from helicopters, girls with bare breasts, girls standing on their heads. For a brief time, the glossy magazines went in for sheer fantasy, because there was nothing else left to do that was different. And this was when Verushka, the tawny, six-foot German countess, came into her own. Verushka was unforgettable as the model girl in Antonioni's film *Blow Up*, but she was more usually to be found on the pages of *Vogue* disguised as some sort of animal or flower—perhaps stencilled all over with tiger stripes and lying along a branch of an African tree, or with her lovely face stuck all around with huge purple petals. It was all very clever but didn't have much to do with the readers or with fashion. American Penelope Tree with her rod-straight hair and stalk-like eyelashes was another eccentric, another natural for bizarre ideas—such as an extraordinary Mickey Mouse wig she once wore for a David Bailey picture.

Since then fashion has changed dramatically, and so have the girls chosen for photographs. The last few years have been like a fantastic fancy dress party at which we have been allowed to wear anything we choose. We have had the baggy army surplus look, the Chinese look, the African look, the Red Indian look, the Peruvian Indian look, the layered look, the Russian peasant look, the cheap chic of secondhand clothes, the Spanish look, and the perennial fad for jeans. The model girls who have succeeded have been the ones with faces strong enough to carry off all these astonishing garments. In a way, this is why the girls of the seventies have more in common with those of the fifties than they do with the models of ten years ago. The new breed have aggressive jawlines, clearly defined brows, strong healthy faces, and they look older than they are. Jerry Hall, a young Texan whose rise to the top was completed by the time she was twenty, and Margaux Hemingway, granddaughter of Ernest, are typical of the seventies girls. It seems to be America's turn to supply top models now, though the exotic faces of Orientals also suit the fancy dress clothes. Marie Helvin, the third Mrs David Bailey, is from Hawaii; she is half-Danish, half-Japanese and wholly beautiful. Being flawless in face and form she can wear anything. Indeed, she does, and her distinctive face is now so familiar to the British public that art directors are known to have implored their fashion editors not to use her. And that, fickle and cruel though it may be, is the surest sign of success in this easily bored business.

Overleaf: Top left: The *Daily Express* feature in 1966 that shot Twiggy to fame and fortune. *Right:* The face that became so familiar. *Below:* Twiggy as she looks now, softer, prettier, altogether different.

153

Twiggy

The Cockney Kid with the face to launch a thousand shapes And she's only 16!

THE GOOD LITTLE GIRL LOOK.
"There was a little girl
and she had a little curl . . ."

by
DEIRDRE McSHARRY

THIS IS THE FACE OF '66 . . . just 16, Cockney-pert and with the stamp of "now." THIS IS THE NAME, Twiggy (yes, really) because she is branch slim, bends to every shape in fashion and has her hair cut like a cap made of leaves.
THIS IS THE LOOK that from this moment will launch thousands of clothes, a craze for freckles, dozens of hairpieces, and cause a sellout in

THE LOLITA LOOK. Long, false plait of fair "hair" to pin on a short hairstyle. It's Twiggy's way. Could be yours—for instant youth.

THE TWIGGY LOOK—lean and bendy—like a tree in winter. Twiggy in her own gear, tight bell-bottoms she made herself and Poor Boy sweater her mother knit for her.

The models of today have a harder look than was fashionable ten years ago. *Left*: Maudie James, a sweet-faced girl who was popular in the sixties (*inset*) has successfully adopted the new, tougher, image. *Above*: Jerry Hall, a Texan beauty whose strong features are perfect for the bizarre clothes of the seventies.

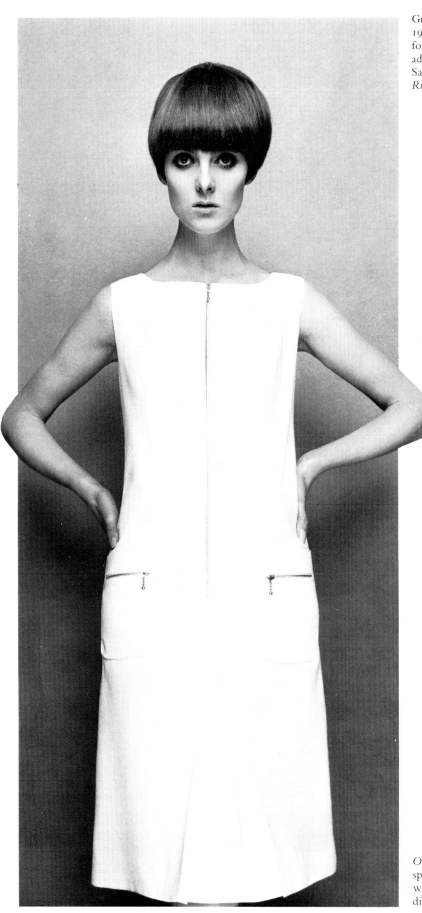

Grace Coddington became a model in 1959 and through the hectic years that followed proved to be astonishingly adaptable. *Left:* In 1965 with a Vidal Sassoon haircut and Mary Quant dress. *Right:* Ten years later and unrecognisable.

Overleaf: Paulene Stone's career has spanned twenty years. By keeping pace with fashion she looks as good now as she did at the start.

10 The Body Bared

In 1970 some wag invented a test by which you could judge whether or not your body was good enough to wear the latest fashion. The test was very simple. It consisted of merely placing a pencil underneath each breast. If the pencils stayed put, you failed; if they dropped out it meant that your bust was firm and upright enough for the fashion, which was, of course, to go braless or even topless. Newspapers named the summer of 1970 'the nudest ever'.

This was the grand finale of a long, slow striptease that had been going on all through the sixties. It started at the very beginning of the decade when we stepped out of our corsets and roll-ons, and the rigmarole of stockings and suspenders was replaced by flesh-coloured tights. Some women found even this early opening move hard to take—the new rounded bellies and bouncing buttocks may have been comfortable, but to them they looked a bit sluttish. To this day my mother thinks we would all look much more attractive if we reverted to what she insists on calling 'stays'. But far worse was to come. In 1964 the Californian designer Rudi Gernreich launched a topless bathing suit. It became the most talked-about, written-about, laughed-about garment of the year, but on the whole it was dismissed as a gimmick and something that could not possibly catch on. 'No girl would wear it,' said an American buyer, 'and if she did the police would run her in.' It strikes me now as curious that the women (including myself) who were so purse-lipped about the topless suit were the very same ones who in the fifties had been quite happy to wear the most unnatural uplift bras in order to force their breasts into twin ice-cream cones. In those days the bigger the bust, the better, but it had to be covered—even if only by a bikini, that revealing swimsuit that had been invented towards the end of the previous decade and named after the atoll where an atomic bomb was tested in 1946. When an ambitious starlet called Simone Silva removed her bra at the 1954 Cannes Film Festival it caused such an uproar that in the stampede to get near her, three photographers fell into the sea, another broke an elbow, and another an ankle. Miss Silva was more or less forced to leave the Festival, condemned as a 'very silly girl'.

Now here we were, ten years later, recoiling in much the same way from the topless suit. *Elle* magazine published a photograph of the outrageous garment with a line of text blotting out the nipples, which read: '*Elle* rejects this: not fashion, not an idea, but a joke.'

Previous page: This picture of the Swiss model Rita illustrated a feature on body jewellery, and was among the earliest nude shots to appear in a respectable British newspaper.

Above left: For a 1969 Elliott's advertisement, Mauritian model Hylette Adolfe wore nothing more than a pair of their boots. *Left:* Three models from the agency Blondes, which specializes in nudes.

Rudi Gernreich's swimsuit was first modelled by his mannequin Peggy Moffatt, a zany girl with crazy eye make-up and a
Vidal Sassoon hair cut, but even she would only pose for her
photographer husband in it. The picture he took now has the
status of an historical document. *Women's Wear Daily* published
it in America (using it rather small) and the paper completely
sold out—even the Editor's own copy was stolen from his
office.

Gernreich's bandwagon was hastily boarded by other
manufacturers, and the topless suit was instantly followed by a
topless cocktail dress. All sorts of versions of these two went
unashamedly on display in shop windows in Britain and
America, though when newspapers talked about them (which
they did incessantly) they photographed the dresses back to
front for modesty's sake, and had sketches done of the swimsuits. Inevitably there were girls who went topless for a bet or
for publicity, and they were, as predicted, run in by the police
every time. Toni Lee Schelley, a nineteen-year-old American
was the first victim, nabbed by the cops as she stepped out of
the sea in her topless suit in California. She was fined £35.
Girls went topless on buses, topless to film premières, topless to
restaurants; and they were duly thrown out on every occasion.
It became repetitive and boring, and Mary Quant's husband
Alexander had, we thought with relief, the last word when he
was quoted as saying, 'They've been taken in, poor things. No
one was actually intended to wear a topless dress . . . it's simply
a caricatured symbol of the fact that busts are in.'

That might have been that, but for Saint Laurent's spring
collection four years later in January 1968. During that show
journalists shot to the very edges of their little gilt chairs when
his redheaded star mannequin Danielle opened the jacket of her
trim culotte suit to reveal that *nom de bleu*! she was wearing a
transparent blouse underneath with no bra. A serious Paris
couturier of the status of Saint Laurent exposing girls' nipples
was different to the eccentric swimsuit designer and his topless
lark. Once again the papers made a meal of it, and *Nova* magazine commissioned a long serious piece from a psychiatrist
called 'The See-Through Dress is a Symptom Not an Epidemic'.
They were wrong. A flood of body jewellery, nipple decorations and body paint came on to the market, along with racks
of see-through blouses (and more arrests for indecency)—
though it should be said that on the whole they were less
popular with the public than they were with the press.

By 1969 naked breasts were uninhibitedly published even in
serious newspapers like the *Sunday Times*, and they were used
(a little less boldly) in all sorts of advertising campaigns, the
most striking in Britain being the posters for Elliott's boots. A
curious by-product of this was the new-found success of
agencies specializing in nudes—after all, someone had to strip off
for these pictures. Annie Walker, who had opened the first nude
agency in London in 1965 without much success ('No one
wanted to know') suddenly found business booming. In 1968

Below: Film starlet Simona Silva caused a
scandal at the Cannes Film Festival in 1954
when she posed, topless, with Robert
Mitchum. *Right:* Ten years later, the
topless bathing suit came into fashion.
Peggy Moffatt posed for this, the very
first photograph of one (designed by Rudi
Gernreich), taken by her husband
William Claxton.

ANNIE WALKER AGENCY
58 Paddington Street London W1   01·486.3625

Donna Reading   Louisa Livingstone   Yvonne Paul

Jane Spearing

Beerla Sector   Vivienne Warren   Mary & Madelaine Collins

Greta

Jasmine Patten   Lucienne Camille   Linda Dean

Brown   Juliet Adams

Sue Bond   Jean   Samantha Bond

Nicola Austine   Maria Frost   Susie

Left: Yves Saint Laurent created the first see-through blouse. It was worn under an evening suit by his red-headed model Danielle. *Above:* Annie Walker opened a nude model agency in London in 1965. Her 'head sheet' was the first to show girls with nothing on.

she produced her first 'head sheet' (a head sheet contains photographs of all the models together with their particulars). Miss Walker's was different to those of other model agencies, for hers showed not only her model's faces but their naked bodies. It was actually not very useful as a head sheet because no sooner was it pinned up on an office wall than someone would steal it. By 1972 there was enough nude work in London to support the opening of another agency, Blondes.

The effect of all this exposure was a definite change in women's shapes. Lots of girls started going braless. The habit was encouraged by Women's Libbers who saw the bra as a sort of symbolic harness and publicly burned theirs 'to demonstrate their disgust and alienation from sexist society'. Even if your bosom was too floppy to let loose, you at least chose a bra that was soft and natural enough to make it look as if you weren't wearing one. Indeed, in 1972, *Elle* magazine told their readers that even breasts 'weighed down with faults or wobbly' were more erotic than those bolstered up artificially.

By the end of the sixties there were topless beaches, topless waitresses, topless go–go dancers, and in March 1971 Britain had the topless *Times*. That newspaper, whose name is a by-word for respectability across the world, astonished its readers when it published a full-page advertisement for Fisons chemicals showing a well-known nude model, Vivian Neaves, kneeling and combing her hair without a stitch of clothing on her. *The Times* didn't go out of business, the world didn't end, and as far as I know, Ms Neaves was not struck down by a thunderbolt. No one even called her a silly girl.

Below: Women's Libber Diana Matthews burns her bra in protest outside the offices of the all-male Magic Circle in London in 1972.

Hand in hand with what was going on in life went the attitudes of our film censors, and their attitudes were similar in Britain and in the United States. In 1925 the British Board of Film Censors had made this comment in a report: 'The Board wishes to deprecate what seems to be a growing habit with actors of both sexes to divest themselves of their clothes on slight, or no, provocation. For instance, in what is a common scene when the heroine is assaulted by the villain, she almost invariably contrives to pull down her dress well off the *shoulders* [my italics].' By the early fifties the Board was allowing the public tiny glimpses of naked bodies, but only 'discreet and distant' and only in *foreign* films with English subtitles. Soon the Board was faced with a rush of films about nudist camps. Nudism, the producers must have thought, was a good clean way of showing naked bodies and getting round the censor. (Schoolboys were on to this already. My husband tells me that *Health and Efficiency*, the British magazine of the nudist movement, was a popular if illicit magazine during his schooldays.) The Board decided to pass nudist films so long as they were 'without pubic hair or genitals being visible and provided that the setting was recognizable as a nudist camp'. This decision was condemned by the *Daily Mirror* who called it AN OUTRAGE TO PUBLIC DECENCY (and of course published stills from the nudist films alongside their protest). By today's

What's a nice girl like you doing in a firm like this?

FISONS

standards the scenes from the nudist pictures are hilariously dated—jolly, cheerful groups of chaps and girls standing behind conveniently-placed gates or fences and looking about as erotic as a pair of old tennis shoes. The censors were admittedly a little anxious; they believed that with the passing of these films nudity would escalate, and so it did, but it was not until 1967 that the last taboo was broken.

The last taboo was, of course, what came to be known as full-frontal nudity: which really meant pubic hair. John Trevelyan was the British Chief Film Censor of the day, and though he first cut the controversial scene, he eventually passed a Swedish film called *Hugs and Kisses* in which for one fleeting moment the heroine looks at the reflection of her naked body, pubic hair and all, in a mirror.

In the autumn of 1968, theatre censorship was lifted altogether in Britain, and immediately the musical *Hair* opened in London (the producers had postponed the first night by two months in order to beat the Censor). *Hair* had opened in New York earlier that year, and its nude scene caused a worldwide furore, which incidentally brought the musical fame and fortune. The press christened the show 'a shocker' and I remember going to see it a few weeks after it opened in London, quaking with nerves as to what I might be forced to watch, and feeling immensely relieved that the stage was so dark that I was hard pressed to catch more than a shadowy glimpse of what was going on.

The following year, Mary Quant valiantly predicted that pubic hair would be something that fashion designers could not

Right: Pubic hair was first shown on the British screen when the film censor passed this shot in a Swedish film called *Hugs and Kisses*.

Overleaf: In the seventies swimsuits have become more and more revealing. This version of The String came into the shops in 1974.

Below: Streaking became a craze in 1974. This girl's streak didn't last long

ignore. She was quoted in *Goodbye Baby and Amen*, a fashionable book of photographs by David Bailey, as saying, 'We shall move towards exposure and body cosmetics and certainly pubic hair—which we can now view in the cinema and on the stage—will become a fashion emphasis, although not necessarily blatant. I think it is a very pretty part of the female anatomy; my husband once cut mine into a heart shape.'

Her daring words hit the headlines, but in a street poll taken among fashionable young girls, incidentally wearing the very minimum of mini skirt, the interviewer found that Miss Quant's words had fallen on deaf ears. The mini-skirted girls all agreed that pubic hair was 'ugly' and said they would certainly not wear any fashion which revealed theirs.

Despite this verdict, it has to be said that swimsuits *have* become more and more revealing. In the last few years we have seen the launching of The Thong, The String and The Savage, and it seems there are women prepared to wear almost anything or, I should say, almost nothing. In the summer of 1976, when I rather nervously featured a swimsuit that had absolutely no covering for the behind at all, the shop who stocked it sold out. And critics of Miss Quant should bear in mind that in 1974 thousands of grown men and women had appeared in public without any clothes on at all. That was the year of streaking mania in which there were parachute streakers, Vatican streakers, a Wall Street streaker, and a record-breaking streak at the University of Georgia, when 1,543 students took off their clothes. Streaking started on the American university campus and its object according to one streaker was 'to be seen by as many people as possible without letting the police catch you with your pants down'. However senseless, the undignified sight of all sizes and shapes of people tearing along in the nude (with their shoes and socks on for speed) did bring smiles to the lips of newspaper readers and television viewers. It also produced some wonderful headlines—my favourite, when thirteen students streaked under the Eiffel tower, was OH LA LA WHAT AN EYEFUL AT THE EIFFEL.

11 How Black Became Beautiful

The oddest woman ever seen in fashion (or out of it for that matter) exploded into the glossy magazines in 1964. Six foot tall, snarling, crouching, hands crooked into claws, eyes rolling —this was Donyale Luna, the first black model girl to become an international star, She crashed through the colour bar that, however unwittingly, had existed in the fashion business.

The six-page feature in American *Harper's Bazaar* that launched her got off to a bad start by captioning the pictures 'as worn by Donyale Luna with all the grace and strength of a Masai warrior'. In a serious article about the problems of the negro working girl, the *New York Herald Tribune* condemned this as prejudice of the worst kind. But that didn't spoil the fact that a sort of breakthrough had been made. Fashion magazines that were quick off the mark booked Ms Luna instantly, and those who missed her cast desperately around for other black girls with similar exotic looks. After her initial stunning appearance one journalist wrote that Donyale Luna was only the tip of an iceberg: 'The iceberg is the completely new image of Negro women . . . the Fashion Negress.'

Now this was a novel idea. Until then, any black person who appeared in a fashion picture was usually there because they'd been popped into the background as a kind of prop. The nearest they had come to fashion itself was when from Paris Courrèges, on launching his new short skirts, announced that he was dedicating them to the negro 'because only the negro knee is perfectly proportioned'. A nice idea in theory, but in practice I doubt if Courrèges and the rest of the Paris couture houses could have named half a dozen black clients between them. Black women could be sexy, sinuous, glamorous; and they could be marvellous entertainers, like the great Josephine Baker who quickened the pulse of Paris in the twenties. But when it came to fashion, or fashion magazines and advertising, black women simply did not exist. They were not considered to have the necessary spending power that publishers and agencies want to exploit.

Josephine Baker was born in a slum in Missouri in 1906, of a Jewish father and a Negro mother. She managed to escape from her appalling background and get to Paris where she scandalized the capital with her erotic dancing and risqué songs. She appeared in the *Revue Nègre* at the Théatre des Champs Elysées, dancing the charleston on a drum, her lovely rounded body decorated with a few ostrich feathers, and wearing only a string of imitation bananas round her snake-hips. They called her 'a

Left: Naomi Sims belonged to the new wave of black model girls – the ones who posed simply as themselves, proving to the world that black is beautiful. *Below:* Josephine Baker was one of the first, and certainly the most glamorous, of all the black entertainers.

danger to civilization'. Miss Baker eventually became a highly respectable and respected champion of civil rights, and adoptive mother to twelve orphan children. But it was her early career tricked out in not much more than feathers, sequins and the famous bananas that made her world famous, the stuff of the white man's sexual fantasies—'a sinuous idol who enslaves and incites all mankind'.

That was one kind of image a black girl could strive for; or she could simply fall back on imitating whatever the current white style of beauty happened to be. For years, Negro girls have literally been through torture in their efforts to achieve a white hairstyle. They used dangerous hot combs to straighten their hair, or chemical solutions like sodium hydroxide or lye, which could burn the hair away altogether if not used correctly (singer Shirley Bassey once sued a company when this happened to her). Or of course, there were white-style wigs that black women wore in order to look 'acceptable'. The same thing applied to cosmetics. There was a vast range of make-up for white girls available, and that was all. Black women had no choice but the wildly unsuitable blue and green shadows for their eyes, and scarlet, orange or pink lipsticks. Be-wigged, heavily made up, with thickets of false lashes and bodies encased in glittering sequin sheaths, The Supremes were a perfect example of how black girls built their glamour around white ideals of beauty. But the Supremes were successful, they were among the very few black heroines or pin-ups, and so theirs was the look longed for by blacks from Brixton to Harlem: there was simply no one else you *could* try to imitate.

Above: The Supremes, with Diana Ross (centre). Before the Afro haircut encouraged black women to be themselves, they had no alternative but to conform to white ideals of beauty, wearing wigs and heavy make-up.

174

So much for the background. Donyale Luna's breakthrough into the glossy magazines meant that from then on a black model might actually have some sort of career in front of her, and indeed, later in the sixties an agency called Black Boys opened in London with *only* black people on their books. Yet extraordinary as she was, Ms Luna did not have a style that other women could adopt. 'She looked more like she was going to attack you,' commented one black girl. White fashion

editors used her and her immediate successors for impact, as freakish clothes-horses on which they could photograph their most outrageous garments. The acceptance of Donyale Luna no doubt boosted the morale of the black community, but she could not give them a look of their own.

That, however, followed fast on her heels. By 1966 the time was right for it, a feeling was in the air, and the Black Power movement was gathering momentum. Much earlier in the decade the black South African singer Miriam Makeba had caused comment when she toured the States wearing no wigs, but with her own hair cropped close. Now a pretty black actress, Cecily Tyson, appeared on television with the same sort of hair cut; short, frizzy and not pretending to be anything else but negroid. The Afro style was born.

The Afro cut was exciting and important, not just because it gave black women a fashion of their own for the very first time, but because it was a symbol of something much deeper, of a new pride in race. The Afro said, 'To hell with you and your white ideals. I'm black and I'm proud of it.' Because of its links with Black Power it was at first considered an aggressive style to adopt. Some airlines, for instance, insisted that their steward-esses should continue to wear wigs on duty. 'Some whites,' said a black girl, 'think that because I have an Afro I'm going to burn their houses down.' But by 1968 the phrase 'Black Is Beautiful' had been coined, and *Women's Wear Daily* were able to write with breathless enthusiasm, 'Suddenly it has become fashionable to be black. Now everybody wants to be a soul sister.'

Black women were more and more in the public eye—not just as entertainers, but as politicians, thinkers, and leaders. In

By 1976 the revival of tribal hair styles was in full swing. *Right:* Patricia Ebigwei, Nigerian actress. *Above:* a white model with a black hairstyle.

that same year, 1968, Shirley Chisholm became the first black woman to be elected to Congress in America, and Coretta King took on the civil rights campaign for which her husband had died. But it was wild-haired Angela Davis who best summed up for the world the new black heroine of the day when in 1972 she went on trial, defiant and beautiful, in California.

The new pride in race brimmed over. It was not long before young whites of both sexes were adopting the Afro—ironically with the aid of wigs and perms when necessary. Then came a revival of tribal hairstyles. Again it was Cecily Tyson who was one of the first to appear with her hair painstakingly plaited into the 'corn row' style. In spite of the fact that a hairdo like that takes several hours to do (the advantage being that it lasts several days) it became popular enough not to turn heads in the streets any more.

In the seventies in Paris, ready-to-wear designers dabbled in all sorts of ethnic African looks, from batik prints and kangas to tribal jewellery. But by far the healthiest sign of the black breakthrough was that by the late sixties a black model girl did not have to look like a freak to find herself bookings. In Donyale Luna's day captions for her pictures said things like 'Is it a plane? No. Is it a bird? Yes. It's Donyale Luna, a way outer-space out-of-sight gal . . .' But in 1969 *Life* magazine were able to put Naomi Sims on their cover with the two words 'Top Model'. This lady was not called upon to growl or claw or crouch, she was accepted for what she was, a beautiful, elegant woman who happened to be black. She has been on the best-dressed list several years running, she wears no freaky clothes but dresses simply in pastel colours or white. She does her hair in a refined version of the Afro and her make-up is natural—no day-glo turquoise on her lids, no pale pink on the lips, but a subtle blend of highlights and dark shadows and a brown-red lipstick. Ms Sims was born in Mississippi in 1949, and has always been committed to her colour: 'Black women have captured the limelight and we are here to stay. The world is looking at us. Being a black female should be considered an asset.' She gave up her successful modelling career in 1973 to start a wig company (black styles for black women and each wig has an African name), and because she remembers the difficulty she had as a young girl finding any sort of sensible advice on hair or make-up, in 1976 she published a tome of a beauty book for black women.

Women like Naomi Sims prove that the battle for black beauty has been fought and won. Now she is concerned that black women should relax about their looks and even pleads for tolerance the other way round. 'If a black woman decides to wear make-up, straighten her hair or wear wigs, this is not necessarily indicative of her being conservative in feminism or in politics. You do not necessarily have to wear *daishikis* to prove you are proud of being black.' Her message is clear. Black women no longer have to be freaks, sexpots—or copies of whites. Neither do they have to wear native costume to emphasize their African origins. They can simply be themselves.

178

Above: Angela Davis, here during her trial in California in 1972, projected the new kind of black beauty.

Right: Donyale Luna, who was the first model to break through the colour bar, wears a metal dress by Paco Rabanne.

Right: Silk organza blouse by
Robert Roma, 7 gns; breast
jewellery by James Wedge at
Top Gear, 2 gns a pair.
Stockists are on page 62

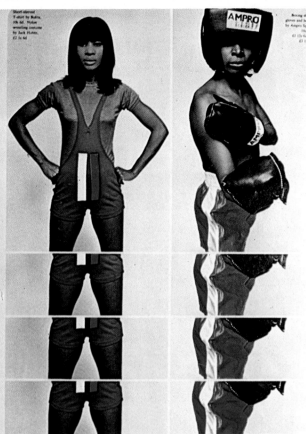

Cotton hat, 6s 9d, racing vest, £2 14s 9d, both by Holdsworth. Cotton training vest, 18s 11d, by Holdsworth, striped cotton hat, 6s 6d, by Holdsworth. Nylon striped racing vest, £2 16s 9d, cotton hat, 6s 6d; embroidered cotton racing vest, £7, striped cotton hat, 6s 6d, all by Holdsworth

Short-sleeved T-shirt by Rubis, 19s 6d. Nylon wrestling costume by Jack Hobbs, £2 1s 6d

Boxing gloves and b by Ampro Sp £2 12s 6d £3 1

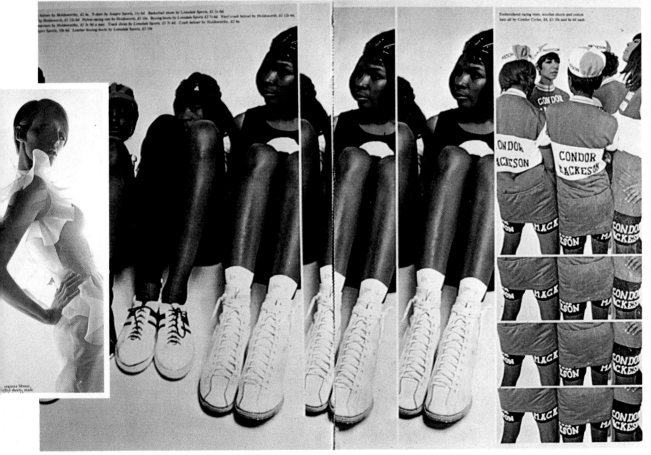

helmet by Holdsworth, £2 4s. T-shirt by Ampro Sports, 11s 6d. Basketball shorts by Lonsdale Sports, £1 1s 6d. by Holdsworth, £1 12s 6d. Nylon racing vest by Holdsworth, £7 10s. Boxing boots by Lonsdale Sports, £2 7s 6d. Vinyl crash helmet by Holdsworth, £5 12s 6d. sweater by Holdsworth, £3 3s 9d a pair. Track shoes by Lonsdale Sports, £2 7s 6d. Crash helmet by Holdsworth, £2 4s. ports, 19s 6d. Leather boxing boots by Lonsdale Sports, £3 10s

Embroidered racing vest, woollen shorts and cotton hats all by Condor Cycles, £4, £3 10s and 6s 6d each

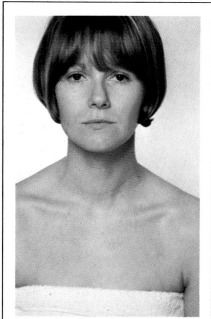

12 Reflections of our Times

Lauren Hutton once described her face as 'lop-sided, cross-eyed, bumpy-nose, and a Huckleberry Finn gap between my two front teeth'. It did not seem to deter the beauty firm Ultima II from wanting Miss Hutton to appear in all their magazine and television advertisements, and in 1973 she agreed a two-year contract with them worth $400,000, making herself the highest paid model girl in history. Not for long, however, for in 1976 the record was broken when Fabergé, another manufacturer, signed up the beautiful, blonde Margaux Hemingway for no less than one million dollars, to promote their new perfume, Babe. (Margaux, incidentally, is so spelt because she was conceived after her parents had consumed a bottle of Chateau Margaux.)

As you might guess from the staggering sums paid to these girls, faces are crucial in beauty advertising. The right ones, it is hoped, will press some secret button in us all, causing us to reach instantly for our purses and *spend*.

In the early days of the cosmetic industry it wasn't enough to choose even the prettiest face for an advertisement: the uncertain public seemed to respond best when the products were endorsed by someone they respected or admired. One of the most famous campaigns was that run by Ponds between the two World Wars.

Ponds persuaded the best-looking society women (who anyway were the ones who then set the trends) to pose for special pictures, and they used their names and their flowery recommendations in advertisements for cold cream. The women were paid, of course, but no stigma seemed to attach itself to the ones who agreed—in fact it was considered quite amusing and chic to be asked to take part. The Ponds' Beauties, as they came to be known, were usually photographed by Shaw Wildman, one of Britain's earliest fashion photographers: 'My aim was to capture something of their natural beauty—an aim not always fully achieved because natural beauty and photogenic beauty are not the same. A beautiful complexion is not easy to reveal in a black and white photograph, it can be destroyed by harsh lighting or poor reproduction. Mistakes could, and often did, haunt one later. They haunt me to this day.' At Wildman's studio Madeleine Constance did the retouching and tried to make every girl a star. To retouch a Ponds' Beauty took a week. 'It was all done on the negative and sometimes we practically had to re-draw them. I remember a Princess who looked so large that we

Previous pages: Nova magazine gained its trend-setting reputation with dynamic fashion pages like these.

Left: Nicole de la Margé, a thoroughly professional model, in half-an-hour could transform her ordinary face (top left) into radiant beauty (below).

183

Pond's became the best-known beauty advertiser between the two World Wars when they persuaded society ladies (like Lady Howe) to endorse their products.

literally had to chop her in half. It always used to irritate me that the ones we'd worked hardest on would ring up when they saw the results and say, "I had no idea how well I photographed. Could I be used for other modelling?"'

After the war, the world had changed and manufacturers no longer needed to attach a grand lady's name to a product before they could sell it. Cosmetics, rather than skin care, were the new thing and Revlon were quick to see that these could be sold successfully if projected with glamour and sex appeal. An early advertisement for a lipstick and nail varnish colour has a raven-haired sophisticate clad in a skintight dress of sequins and the legend, 'Are *You* Made for Fire and Ice?'; the accompanying quiz must have seemed quite daring at the time: 'Do you close your eyes when you're kissed? Do you blush when you find yourself flirting? Do you secretly hope that the next man you meet will be a psychiatrist?' Revlon spared no expense on their advertisements, using top photographers like Richard Avedon, top model girls (especially the beautiful sisters Suzy Parker and Dorian Leigh), and placing them, in full colour, across double-page spreads in magazines. They set the style for all their competitors.

Recently an American psychiatrist had some fun studying nineteen years of Revlon advertisements to see what he could deduce about the moods of their times. From Fire and Ice in 1952 until the end of the sixties, the message came through clearly—we had sex on our minds, and what is more, sex without marriage. In his opinion a 1969 lipstick advertisement was the most blatant—'the woman looks as though she has just been sexually satiated'. But in 1972, Revlon allowed sex to give way to women's liberation, with Jean Shrimpton posing aggressively on a motorcycle. In 1974 the Revlon girl settled down and in advertisements for their new perfume, Charlie, she is strolling along in a trouser suit and in the words of the psychiatrist, looks 'modern, self-assured, liberated'. Revlon never went in for crazy, gimmicky ads, so the psychiatrist never caught a glimpse of the kind that Mary Quant Cosmetics excelled at: eye-catching copy with startling pictures (once just a giant pair of lips across two pages).

Once in a while, an advertisement from a quite unexpected source sums up the mood or the fashion of the moment better than one specifically designed to do so. One would not have expected the National Dairy Council to create a pin-up, but they did in 1954 when they picked a young model girl with a blonde fringe and a cute face because they thought she best embodied 'the spirit of calcium', and photographed her sipping milk through a straw. Her name was Zoë Newton and she became famous as Britain's first public teenager in almost less time than it took to paste up the hoardings.

Magazines, no less than advertisements, have reflected our changing roles and aspirations. Before the War a woman was a socialite (and a reader of the glossies) or she was a housewife, enjoying a diet of home hints, recipes, knitting patterns and stories. But in 1944 at least one new kind of magazine buyer was recognized—the teenager. In the autumn of that year *Seventeen* was launched just for her. I can remember in the fifties saving up my pocket money to buy the occasional copy of *Seventeen*. It was so glossy, so different, so much more *understanding* than any publication produced in Britain. All things American were wonderful in those days and we dreamed about the barbecues, the open convertibles driven by 'dates', but most of all we drooled over the clothes. American girls

seemed to us so fresh with their pony tails and flat pumps, in bobby sox, pedal-pusher jeans, or full skirts with stiff paper nylon petticoats to make them stick out.

A year later, *Elle* magazine appeared on the bookstalls in France. *Elle* was not, like *Seventeen*, exclusively for teenagers, but it certainly recognized their existence—one of their earliest models was an adorable girl whose kittenish face and slim body looked perfect in the rather sickly fashions for girls her age. She was Brigitte Bardot—such an unknown quantity that they never even bothered to put her name in the captions.

Elle was really aimed at another new group of women, the young working girls from middle-class backgrounds who, before the war, had simply stayed at home. These girls were earning money now, they were independent and interested in all aspects of life, including how to dress attractively on a limited budget. *Elle* magazine showed them how even a jumper and skirt and shoulder bag could look chic. The *Elle* style became vastly influential not only on readers, but on manufacturers and fashion writers too. I remember when I worked on the *Daily Express* in the late fifties, that *Elle*'s ideas were very often our inspiration.

One model girl in particular summed up the *Elle* look. She was Nicole de la Margé, perhaps the greatest photographic model of all time; a girl who worked with dazzling professionalism. Nicole started modelling in the mid-fifties when she got a job as a tea-girl-cum-typist-cum-model at a wholesale dress house in Paris. The Fashion Editor of *Jardin des Modes* spotted her 'good bones' and in no time she was on their cover. 'I was lucky. The age of the aloof model was over, everyone was mad about *Seventeen* magazine in the States and I was the anti-Suzy Parker—the girl next door could look like me.' Soon *Elle* magazine adopted her, Peter Knapp the magazine's art director became her boyfriend and by unwritten agreement Nicole only worked for them. 'I lived, breathed and thought the magazine,'

Chanelascopic view of Spring—this year's Chanel suit is a dead simple (of course) two-piece dress, here in **SPARKLING WHITE** tweed sharpened with navy blue braid and softened with bobble fringing.

BE AT THE

wear the covered up look, legs excepted. Mauve silk knitted suit, left, by Irene Galitzine, 25 gns. at Harvey Nichols. Tri-colour straw hat, £3 19s. 6d. at Harrods.

SWEATER SWIM-SUIT

in bright white Helanca, right, 5 gns. at Pia of Venice, South Molton Street. Straw-hatted scarf, £1 9s. 6d. at Woolland's.

B eating the beatnicks at their own game of how to be casually with it.
Three: Cotton shirtwaister in black and white stripes, made to measure at Boutique Hartnell, Brook Street, W.1.
Right: Remember *Les Maîtres de la Nuit* . . . t-shirt in t-shirt tricot . . . By Digby Morton, 6d. Riddlan, £3 19s. 6d. from Boutique Hartnell, W.1.

The country girl gets carried away

Gone: the down-to-earth image of a country girl in sensible clothes. Arrived: revolutionary ideas in out-of-town clothes to make in-town girls look twice. *Left*, a full-length belted coat in supple tawny brown suede, 19 gns. at Suedecraft, Beauchamp Place, and Leith Street, Edinburgh. Centre, low-belted coat, softly fitting, in warm red and black flecked tweed. By Allen Montrose, about £6 gns. at Ivor Hartnell (from August 10th). Dark blue and plum man's Paisley silk scarf, by Hardy Amies, £2 9s. 6d. at Harrods. *Right*, dark dapplegrey and white herring-bone tweed coat, low belt, deep pockets. By Mortessa, 14 gns. Bamboo-coloured pure silk scarf, 1 gn. Both at Woolland's.

photographs by Norman Parkinson

Queen magazine looked quite unlike the other, more conventional glossies of the late fifties. This selection of spreads shows how photographer Norman Parkinson and Art Director

ATNIKS

clothes for Summer, 1960
lay over eighteen. By Horrockses, 6' gns

nile pyjama striped Bonsoir cotton
g Breton, by Chez Elle, 10 gns, at Liberty

Mark Boxer managed to
inject their fashion pages
with wit and excitement.
They chose their model girls
because they looked like real
women and not like super-
sophisticated clothes-horses.

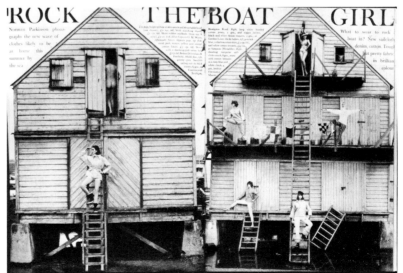

ROCK THE BOAT GIRL

she said. At one unbelievable moment—unbelievable because a model girl was never taken so seriously at that time—it was suggested that Nicole should attend the Paris collections and help choose the clothes they would photograph. 'After all,' explained the Editor to her sulking fashion staff—'this girl IS *Elle* magazine.'

Nicole de la Margé was quite plain without make-up, but given half an hour or so with her bag of cosmetics she could transform her funny little face and mousy hair into things of astonishing beauty. She knew all the tricks of her trade and was constantly changing, adapting, and bringing herself in line with the current fashions. It was Nicole who invented the craze for false freckles when she posed for a holiday cover picture, thinking they would add just the right sunny touch. She even went through the agony of learning to wear contact lenses so that she would be able to alter the colour of her eyes from brown to blue. More than all that, however, Nicole understood clothes, and how to project them to their best effect. She would try everything on before the photograph was taken, and run through a sort of dress rehearsal, picking out accessories, trying them on in different ways, rejecting them for others. The Fashion Editor was redundant when she was the model. 'My only quality,' she once said, 'is to be right for the clothes.'

By 1965 Nicole felt stifled by her *Elle* image, so she escaped to England to try something different. To her horror she found that all the English editors wanted was the *Elle* look, so after two years of frustration she returned to Paris and married a *Paris Match* journalist. Not long afterwards she was tragically killed in a car accident.

American girls had *Seventeen*, the French had *Elle*, but British women had to wait for years for a publication that filled the gap between the glossies and the housewives' magazines (known in the business as the 'Knit-Your-Own-Royal-Family' type). In 1957, Jocelyn Stevens bought the famous socialite magazine *Queen*, and transformed it slowly from a staid Establishment journal, into the bible of the new Chelsea swinger. Norman Parkinson was brought in to take the fashion pictures and was allowed to indulge his wildest ideas. Young models were found (notably Celia Hammond) who looked and posed like real girls. Norman Parkinson, whose eccentricities once ran to photographing the Paris collections on a set of triplets, feels that '*Queen* was most important, for it puts its fingers to its nose at the whole fashion pomposity and beat it open'. Mark Boxer was the Art Director responsible for *Queen*'s exciting layouts: 'We were cocky young men, terribly amateurish. When it came to fashion we simply put in the kind of girls we fancied wearing the sort of clothes we liked. It worked then because everything else was a bit stuffy and stuck, but I don't think we'd be so arrogant now.'

Queen reigned until the advent of yet another new magazine, *Nova*, in 1965. *Nova* coincided with the growing Womens'

Right: Seventeen was the first magazine to recognize the teenager. On this cover the model is Dolores Hawkins.

Overleaf: Revlon advertisements. Left: Fire and Ice, 1952. *Above right:* Jean Shrimpton, aggressive on a motor bike, 1972. *Below:* Cherries in the Snow, 1953 (the model is Dorian Leigh).

seventeen

OCTOBER 1953
35 CENTS IN U.S. AND CANADA
40 CENTS ELSEWHERE

THE
SEVENTEEN
LOOK
and ways
to have it

for you who love to flirt with fire...

who dare to skate on thin ice...

Revlon's 'Fire and Ice'

for lips and matching fingertips. A lush-and-passionate scarlet
...like flaming diamonds dancing on the moon!

"Indelible-Creme" Lipstick...Regular Lipstick
Frosted Nail Enamel...
Improved-Formula Nail Enamel.

Revlon says Vro-o-o-m!
Here they come.
The brights. The bolds.
And the beautifuls.

The
Wild Satins

4 bright, clean, whizzy colors. Chic.
Sexy. Shock-full of shine. For the get-
around-girls who read fashion like a
roadmap. (They've left the pow-less
pales behind!) So where are they
heading? To these racy, revved-up
brights. With a great big luster like
lamps in the rain. Roaring in from
Revlon. The one with the track record.

Fuchsia Shock!

Orange Crash!

Daredevil Pink!

Revlon
Lustrous Lipstick
(Nail enamel to match? Natch!)

Zoomzoom Brown!

Does any man really understand you?

Who knows you as you really are? Does he?
Who knows the secret hopes that warm your heart?
Who knows the dreams you dream, the words you've left unspoken?
Who knows the black-lace thoughts you think while shopping in a gingham frock?
Who knows you sometimes long to sleep in pure-silk sheets?
Who knows you'd love to meet a man who'd hold your hand and listen . . .
     while you say nothing at all?
Who knows there was a morning when your orange juice sparkled like champagne?
Who knows the secret, siren side of you that's female as a silken cat?

*Who else but Revlon understands you as you really are . . .
     a trifle shy, but oh-so-warm . . . and just a little reckless,
deep inside . . . as strange and unexpected as cherries in the snow.*

Revlon's 'Cherries in the Snow'

Non-Smear Lipstick
Regular Lipstick
New! 'Chips-Less'
Nail Enamel

new madly voluptuous scarlet for lips and matching fingertips

queen
has triplets

26 February   Fortnightly 2s 6d

in Paris

Left: One of Norman Parkinson's more
eccentric ideas for *Queen* magazine was
(in 1964) to photograph the Paris
collections on the American Dee triplets.

Overleaf: Nova enjoyed the unexpected.
These two photographs illustrated beauty
features on slimming and ageing.

Liberation movement and like it, it was aggressive, broke the rules, and demanded to be taken seriously. Dennis Hackett edited the magazine in its boom days, and he hired an eccentric, untried Welsh painter called Molly Parkin to do the fashion pages. His gamble paid off. Ms Parkin's pages constantly broke new ground: she made fashion out of clothes from sports shops, from army surplus stores; she photographed girls in bed with men, girls undressing on the beach, girls who looked like lesbians; and she liked plastic and paper better than silk and satin, and clashing colours more than mix-and-match.

Nova's model girls were either chosen because they looked sexy, like Greta Norris with her kissable lips and swelling bosom, or because they were ugly. For by the end of the sixties realism in fashion had become all the rage—so much so, that a new model agency specializing in only odd-looking people was born. Ugly opened in 1969 and their star was Jenny Gaylor, a girl with a broken nose, negroid lips and a long face who, nonetheless, made a highly successful career out of modelling.

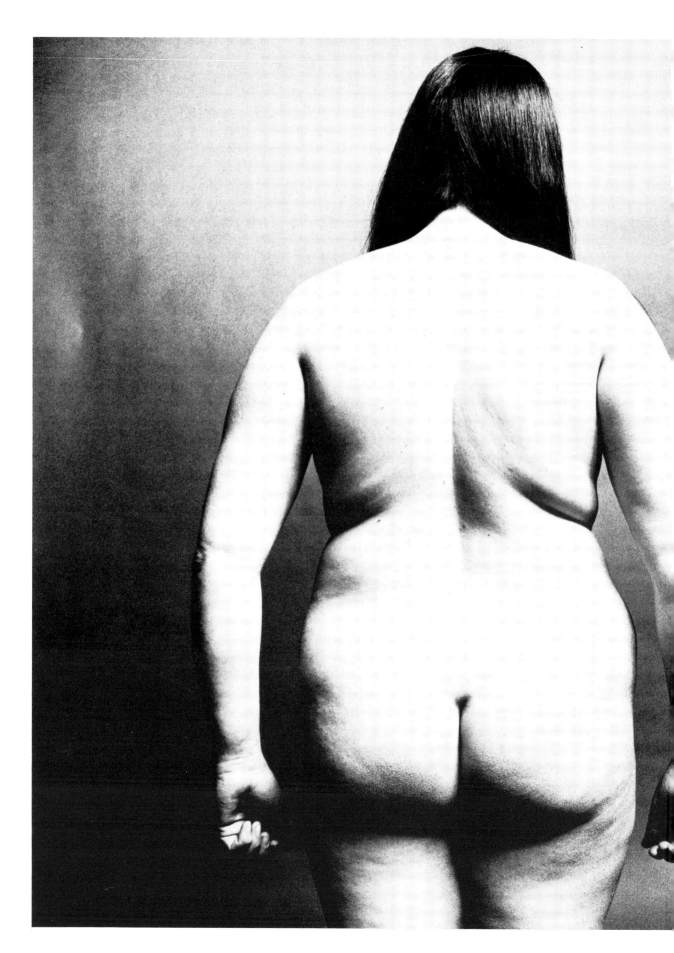

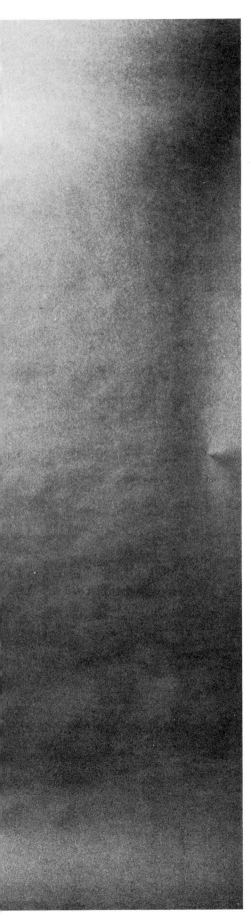

Ugly's stars have also included Fran Fullenwider, a vastly fat but jolly girl, and Jeanette Charles, whose only claim to fame is her uncanny likeness to The Queen.

In 1965 more publishing history was made in America again. Helen Gurley Brown, an attractive 43-year-old fresh from the success of her book *Sex and the Single Girl,* was given the task of reviving a dying magazine. *Cosmopolitan* had been in existence since the end of the nineteenth century as a story magazine, but like most of its kind, its circulation had fallen over the years to a critical low. Helen Gurley Brown was put in charge and the revamped magazine took off from her very first issue. It now has an American circulation of nearly two million; the British edition (launched in 1972) sells half a million.

American *Cosmo* gained its name (and its circulation) by the frank way in which it encouraged readers to enjoy the new sexual freedom—though to be fair most editions, especially British *Cosmo,* take life more seriously these days. Back in the sixties a journalist wrote sourly that Ms Gurley Brown was 'demonstrating that there are over one million American women who are willing to read *not* about politics, *not* about the female liberation movement, *not* about the war in Vietnam, but

merely about how to get a man.' *Cosmo* features are enticingly blurbed on the cover: 'Why I Wear My False Eyelashes to Bed', 'How To Make A False Bosom Amount to Something', 'How To Survive The First Love Affair after Divorce'.

Ms Gurley Brown's philosophy, she maintains, is to help all women achieve at least some of the glamour, if not the status, that she herself found through dedication and hard work. 'If you're a little mouseburger, come with me. I was a mouseburger and I will help you. You're so much more wonderful than you think.' *Cosmo* model girls are handsome healthy types with strong faces and an independent air—they certainly do not look like mouseburgers.

One of the most accurate reflections of our ever-changing ideals of beauty is the shop window dummy. It, or perhaps I should say she, has followed fashion closely over the years, from the early days when mannequins were waxworks with fixed and glassy stares and sinister little teeth made by dentists, to the stylish plaster egg-heads that became all the rage after the Paris Exhibition of 1925, ending up (so far at least) as the lifelike, almost human creatures we are familiar with today.

The most famous dummy ever made was the forerunner of these. She was created in 1937 by Lester Gaba, an American sculptor and designer who based her on a real model girl, Grace Wells. Gaba christened his sophisticated, size 12, papier-maché mannequin Cynthia, and she first appeared in a window at Saks, in New York's Fifth Avenue. Cynthia was considered so astonishingly lifelike that she became a positive craze—aided and abetted by Mr Gaba, who took her to nightclubs and

Previous page: Jenny Gaylor was an early Ugly model, whose unconventional face was her fortune.

Fashionable window dummies in the twenties were stylized egg-heads like the one (left) designed by Marie Laurencin.

Above: A realistic 1976 mannequin based on the Japanese model Sayoko.

parties (she travelled sitting on the floor of taxis) and posed her, dressed in a long evening frock, by the piano in his home where she acted as a kind of unofficial hostess. Cynthia journeyed all over America and Europe and once to Australia, making star appearances in shop windows, and in planes and trains she sat in her own seat just like a real person. She appeared on television and on radio programmes, she took part in the film *Artists and Models* with Jack Benny and Joan Bennett, and was featured in magazine and newspaper articles. Most peculiar of all, Cynthia actually received fan letters, and once in Baltimore, an orchid

was found in front of the window in which she was appearing. Alas, when the more square-shouldered silhouette became fashionable in the forties Cynthia's career was over. She retired to adorn the window of a provincial beauty parlour where, one day in 1945, she fell off a chair and broke.

In 1961 Adel Rootstein started making mannequins (she will never consent to call them dummies) which, like Cynthia, were based on real and recognizable women. Miss Rootstein has an uncanny knack of spotting the faces that will set the fashions. She was making Twiggies and black Donyale Lunas as soon as their first pictures appeared in the papers. She made a Joanna Lumley before the real one signed her contract to appear in *The Avengers* television series, and she had a Marie Helvin before that model became famous 'Sometimes I seem to bring them luck,' smiled Miss Rootstein.

She always has lots of mannequins in the pipeline, men and children, as well as women, but currently the face she is most intrigued by is that of the Japanese model, Sayoko. 'She has a quality of mystery,' she says, 'something that is simply non-existent in other girls at the moment.' Miss Rootstein's mannequin of Sayoko was released to stores and shops across the world in 1976, but in her opinion that is only a small part of the fame yet to come to this oriental beauty.

13 The Outsiders

When I was a fashion editor I was occasionally cornered at parties by grim-faced women who seemed to see me as some kind of undercover agent for the clothing manufacturers. My main job, they implied, was simply to keep hemlengths and waistlines moving up and down as often as possible, in order to keep the readers spending more and more money. My assailants always mentioned platform-soled shoes as a typical example of the senseless, even dangerous, fripperies that fashion writers could make popular by a mere tap on the typewriter.

To prove that women are not so easily swayed, I would tell of the notorious winter of 1969 when the entire rag-trade turned out midi-length coats because that was the fanfared new fashion from Paris, and then were left holding them at the end of the season because shoppers passed them by. As for platform-soled shoes, they continued to be best-sellers long after the editors had confidently announced they were OUT. And what about the column inches devoted every summer to 'The Return of the Mini Skirt'—news to which most newspaper readers have over the years steadfastly turned a blind eye.

Fashion cannot be forced on anyone. Its ways are perverse and unpredictable, and what proves that beyond all doubt is the fact that some of its most influential figures have been women who cared not one jot about it. Trends that have affected us all have been born on the backs of women too poor to buy proper clothes, too busy to think about them, or too independent to care about convention. Instead of being handed down to us, literally ready-made, from the authoritative heights of the couture houses or the best-dressed lists, these ideas have sprung up spontaneously from the streets, as it were, and they have always found a ready audience among students and young people, for whom dressing controversially is an essential part of the generation game. Clothes are one of the most effective ways of proclaiming that you don't give a damn about your elders and their stifling, rule-ridden society.

The Second World War produced a predictable backlash among young people desperate to prove that they were no part of the generation that had led the world into chaos. From 1945 for more than a decade, any self-respecting rebel cultivated a face as white and unhealthy-looking as a plant forced in the dark, and wore a uniform composed of a baggy black sweater, tight jeans, sandals, and unkempt long hair. These youngsters came to be called beatniks, but their style was originally in imitation of Juliette Greco, a French singer who looked poor,

Brigitte Bardot's kittenish face and long-limbed body persuaded *Elle* magazine to choose her as one of their young fashion models long before she became famous.

shabby and half-starved because indeed she had been all those things, a piece of flotsam cast up by the tide of the War.

Juliette Greco was fifteen years old when her mother and sister were arrested by the Germans in Paris and deported. Miserable, homeless and frightened, she tried to get herself locked up with them, but failed because of her age. A friend of her mother provided shelter and sent young Juliette to an acting school where she became part of a group of students who had so little money they often went hungry. They wore their hair long because they could not afford visits to the hairdresser, they wore black jerseys because they did not show the dirt, and men's trousers or jeans because they had no cash for stockings. In occupied Paris their hunger for liberty and independence found release in the writings of poets and philosophers, in earnest discussion and the constant exchange of ideas.

After the Liberation, the group took to meeting for their talks in a bistro which conveniently stayed open all night, called the Tabou in Saint Germain des Près. It did not take them long to discover that there was an unused cellar below the restaurant, and eventually they moved in there and turned it into a kind of club where they could talk undisturbed. Members of the group provided music or sang, and soon the place started attracting attention. Jean-Paul Sartre, the existentialist philosopher visited the cellar, and after that a journalist christened the whole group 'existentialists'—they were proud of Sartre's patronage and did not deny it. Negro musicians from Harlem came to play for them, *Life* magazine did a four-page feature on them, and their club became the most talked-about place in Paris—and one of the most exclusive, because the group were choosey and closed their doors to the merely curious, the sensation-seekers or the rich and wealthy who thought it fun to slum it for an evening. Juliette Greco, so poor but so beautiful, who sang so sadly but with such soul, became famous and the idol of a generation whose childhood, like hers, had been tarnished by war. All over Europe and America young people grew their hair, dressed in Greco's black sweater and jeans, and chose to congregate in cellar clubs that throbbed with beat music. 'Saint Germain des Près', said André Maurois, 'conquered the world without ever having thought of doing so.'

Dorelia McNeill was just as unlikely a fashion source as Juliette Greco, but through the paintings and drawings of her that hang in art galleries all over the world, her unique way of dressing has influenced us for seventy-odd years. For this secret and serene woman, despite some turbulent ups and downs, was the life-long love and inspiration of the painter Augustus John.

No stylish woman had ever dared before to dress as Dorelia did. She ignored conventional fashion absolutely, and yet for three decades before the last war she *was* the fashion in artistic circles. Anyone who pretended to be the least bit Bohemian wore their hair chopped short the way Dorelia did, they copied her peasant clothes, her smocks and her simple dirndl skirts.

Juliette Greco's enormous influence on the way young people dressed came about by accident. She wore drab sweaters and trousers not merely for effect, but because they were all she could afford.

And when, in the sixties, Laura Ashley's long cotton dresses became the uniform for young girls they were only an echo of the style Dorelia set so long ago.

Dorelia was born Dorothy McNeill in nowhere more exotic than Camberwell, in South London. She was the daughter of a mercantile clerk, became a typist in a solicitor's office and went to art classes in the evenings. Somewhere, somehow (no one knows exactly) she met Augustus John in 1903 when she was twenty-two. She was astonishingly beautiful in a dark and mysterious way, with high cheekbones and slanting eyes, and to emphasize her unconventional look, Augustus John dressed her in straw hats and simple peasant dresses that reached the ankles. He wove such an aura of mystery around her, in fact, that many people believed that Dorelia was really a gypsy girl. That is how he liked her to look, and that is how he painted her, and through those paintings her influence was enormous. She was, in a way, the original hippy.

Surrounded by children in a rambling house with a wild garden, Dorelia lived the life that went with the clothes. Her kitchen smelled of newly-baked bread, piles of home-grown produce lay about, earthenware jars brimmed with cream or home-made mead, and flowers overflowed everywhere.

This delicious picture of self-sufficient bliss in the unspoilt depths of the countryside is what the city-dweller yearns for now more than ever before. It is what drop-outs are dreaming of when they leave the rat-race, and for those of us left in the concrete jungles, it finds release in fads like health foods and home-baking. When in 1965 the first hippies emerged from the

Left: In the sixties even well-born young people like Jane Ormsby-Gore deliberately flouted the conventions of their elders by wearing an odd assortment of clothes from junk shops and secondhand stalls. *Right:* In 1967 the Beatles' wives took to wearing hippy clothes. From left to right: Patti Harrison, Cynthia Lennon and Maureen Starr. In front: Patti's sister Jenny.

crumbling Victorian houses of Haight Ashbury, San Francisco, it was this same paradise of love and peace that they preached.

The first flower child I met had become noticed in Britain because she was such an unlikely recruit to the new movement that was sweeping Europe and America and sending tendrils out as far as India and Nepal. Jane Ormsby-Gore was the daughter of Lord Harlech, and no one had heard of her until in 1966, when she was twenty-three, she married Michael Rainey, the owner of a trendy Chelsea boutique called Hung On You, and went to her wedding in a secondhand Victorian dress that had middle-aged matrons all over Britain clucking with disapproval. Mrs Rainey, it was felt, was rather letting the side down; but worse was to come. She had a son and named him Saffron, she spoke out openly against the restrictive drug laws —'I think marijuana is probably far less damaging than all the pills people seem to take'—she wore the oddest clothes, a

In the fashion world today, anything goes. *Left:* Caroline Baker in sarong and gold shoes. *Right:* Designer Wendy Dagworthy in hacking jacket. *Far right:* Public relations consultant Lynne Franks in baggy shirt and jeans.

mixture of secondhand twenties and thirties dresses, gaudy jewellery and trendy bell-bottom trousers, and though the Raineys lived in an elegant house in Westminster surrounded on all sides by respectable members of Parliament, it contained hardly any furniture but was filled with the monotonous drone of Indian music and the sweet smell of incense and joss sticks.

Eventually the Raineys took the next step and dropped out altogether, but by that time they were just part of a big untidy crowd, and though older people never lost their distaste for the undisciplined way the hippies dressed and lived, Flower Power and Love-Ins had lost their shock value and by 1967 the most blinkered office worker could hum the melodic hit song that told us 'If you go to San Francisco be sure to wear some flowers in your hair'.

In that year of 1967 I met a group of young Dutch fashion designers who made Jane Rainey look positively dull. To my

Anna Piaggi, an Italian fashion
editor. *Right:* Eccentric dressers like
designer Zandra Rhodes have helped to
tear down all the old fashion taboos.

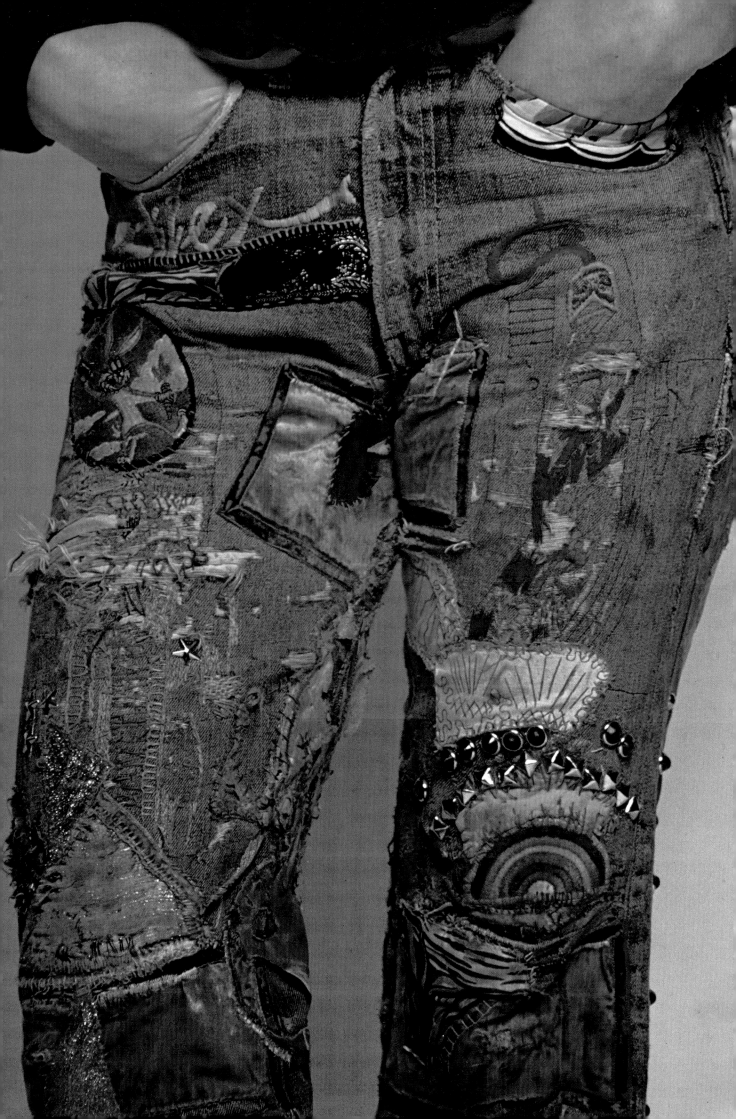

middle-class eye they seemed like creatures from outer space, and to tell the truth I was really rather frightened of them. They had been set up in business by the Beatles—brought in to be part of their Apple enterprises—and the Beatle wives, who up until then had been quite conventional little women, suddenly adopted the long skirts, peacock colours and shimmering silks and satins and embroideries that the Apple designers gloried in.

By that time there were two kinds of hippy. There were the genuine ones in faded jeans, sandals, and beads on leather thongs, who straggled off on roads leading East, or congregated in groups anywhere they felt they might be left alone—Ibiza, Amsterdam, even on the beach at St Ives, Cornwall. And then there were the more fashionable hippies who revelled in the uninhibited new clothes, and scarves, and necklaces, and hair-dos, smoked a bit of pot, but never really dropped out. The travelling hippies sometimes funded their long journeys by bringing back the kind of colourful garments and jewellery the stay-at-home hippies would pay good money for.

By their rejection of materialism—which included mass-produced modern clothes—the hippies had a profound effect on fashion. They injected it with colour, taught us not to be afraid of mixing prints and patterns, and piling on lots of jewellery. They gave people a feeling for natural fibres, hand-work and embroidery, and a new taste for ethnic ideas. At first this was limited to all things Indian, but within a few years it embraced the whole world to include ponchos from Peru, sarongs from Bali, kaftans from Morocco and so on. Not least, by adopting jeans as part of their uniform, they engulfed Europe and America in a tidal wave of blue denim. The hippies gave us a new standard to dress by: now clothes did not have to look suitable, expensive or chic, they simply had to be decorative.

All this was incomprehensible to a lot of people and the generation gap in fashion would have widened, if the new, more romantic, way of dressing had not struck a chord in some respected fashion designers and editors. Through them, it has influenced us all, although not too many of us, I suspect, would wish to go to the extremes that fashion people get away with simply by virtue of being in the business up to their necks.

Not long ago I did a story on what women involved in the rag trade were wearing themselves, and I must say I was a little startled when they turned up to be photographed. There was a stylist in army surplus jodhpurs, shirt and tie, a designer with bright green hair, and Caroline Baker, a fashion writer, wore her battered old jeans with high-heeled gold shoes, a sarong, and her hair slicked down with gooey gel. In Italy, Anna Piaggi, a fashion editor on Italian *Vogue*, is an In person despite—or perhaps because of—the odd way she dresses her short and tubby figure. She collects old clothes from the great designers, and will wear, for instance, a 1920s Jean Patou black sable coat with a bit of net round her neck and gold mesh gloves from Barkers in Kensington. She was seen at a Paris show last year in a

gardening apron complemented by a pair of gardening gloves, and she once attended the collections wearing Marks & Spencer bedroom slippers. In America, Caterine Milinaire, who is the Duke of Bedford's stepdaughter and an ex-*Vogue* fashion editor, co-authored an anti-fashion book at the end of 1975 called *Cheap Chic*, in which she instructed readers in the art of looking good in army surplus, secondhand clothes, workman's overalls, sportswear—she talked about all clothes in fact, except the ones women were likely to find in their local stores. *Cheap Chic* sold a quarter of a million copies within a few weeks.

In the way that tiny drops of water can wear away solid stone, the bizarre influence over the years of women like Dorelia John, Juliette Greco, Marquesa Casati and Zandra Rhodes, and of groups such as beatniks and hippies, has erased all the rules in fashion. For the moment, at least, we can enjoy the heady freedom of knowing that anything goes.

Bibliography

Anderson Black, J. and Garland, Madge, *A History of Fashion* (Orbis, London 1975)

Antoine, *Antoine* (W. H. Allen, London—date unknown)

Bailey, David, and Evans, Peter, *Goodbye Baby & Amen* (Condé Nast Publications Ltd. Coward, McCann, USA 1969)

Ballard, Bettina, *In My Fashion* (Martin Secker & Warburg, 1960)

Beaton, Cecil, *Cecil Beaton's Scrapbook* (Batsford Press, London 1937)

——*The Glass of Fashion* (Weidenfeld & Nicolson, London 1954)

——*Cecil Beaton's Diaries: The Wandering Years 1922–1939; The Years Between 1939–1944; The Happy Years, 1944–1948; The Strenuous Years, 1948–1955* (Weidenfeld & Nicolson, London 1961, 1965, 1972, 1973)

——*Fashion, an anthology* (HMSO, London 1971)

Bell, Quentin, *On Human Finery* (The Hogarth Press, London 1947, revised 1976)

Carter, Randolf, *The World of Flo Ziegfeld* (Elek, London 1974)

Channon, Sir Henry, *Chips, the Diaries of Sir Henry Channon* (Weidenfeld & Nicolson, London 1967)

Charles-Roux, Edmonde, *Chanel* (Cape, London 1976)

Chase, Edna and Ilka, *Always in Vogue* (Gollancz, London 1964)

Chierichetti, David, *Hollywood Costume Design* (Studio Vista, London 1976)

Clayton, Lucie, *The World of Modelling* (Harrap, London 1968)

Cooper, Lady Diana, *The Rainbow Comes and Goes; The Light of Common Day; Trumpets from the Steep* (Hart Davis, London 1958, 1959, 1960)

Donaldson, Frances, *Edward VIII* (Weidenfeld & Nicolson, London 1974)

Dorner, Jane, *Fashion in the Twenties and Thirties* (Ian Allen, London 1973)

——*Fashion* (Octopus, London 1974)

——*Fashion in the Forties and Fifties* (Ian Allen, London 1975)

Fairchild, John, *The Fashionable Savages* (Doubleday, USA 1965)

Fielding, Daphne, *Emerald & Nancy* (Eyre & Spottiswoode, London 1968)

Ford, Eileen, *Secrets of the Model's World* (Trident Press, USA 1970)

Gabor, Mark, *The Pin-Up* (André Deutsch, London 1972)

Garland, Madge, *The Changing Face of Beauty* (Weidenfeld & Nicolson, London 1957)

——*The Indecisive Decade* (Macdonald, London 1968)

——-*The Changing Form of Fashion* (Dent, London 1970)

Haedrich, Marcel, *Coco Chanel* (Hale, USA 1972)

Holroyd, Michael, *Augustus John* (Heinemann, London 1974)

Idea Books in association with Scottish Arts Council and Victoria & Albert Museum, *Fashion 1900–1939* (Idea Books, London 1975)

Lambert, Eleanor, *The World of Fashion* (Bowker, USA 1976)

Leese, Elizabeth, *Costume Design in the Movies* (B.C.W. Publishing, USA 1976)

Lynam, Ruth, ed. *Paris Fashion* (Michael Joseph, London 1972)

Margaret, Duchess of Argyll, *Forget Not* (W. H. Allen, London 1975)

Margetson, Stella, *The Long Party* (Gordon Cremonesi, London 1974)

Maurois, André, *The Women of Paris* (Bodley Head, London 1954)

Milinaire, Caterine, and Troy, Carol, *Cheap Chic* (Harmony Books, USA 1976)

Pignatelli, Luciana, *The Beautiful People's Beauty Book* (McCall, USA 1970)

Quant, Mary, *Quant by Quant* (Cassell, London 1966)

Sassoon, Vidal, *Sorry I Kept You Waiting Madam* (Cassell, London 1968)

Shrimpton, Jean, *The Truth about Modelling* (W. H. Allen, London 1964)

Spanier, Ginette, *It Isn't All Mink* (Collins, London 1959)

Tomkins, Calvin, *Living Well is the Best Revenge* (André Deutsch, London 1972)

Trevelyan, John, *What the Censor Saw* (Michael Joseph, London 1973)

Twiggy, *Twiggy, an autobiography* (Hart Davies MacGibbon, London 1975)

Elle

Sunday Times

Women's Wear Daily

Index

Photographic Sources

Front jacket, courtesy Revlon; **Back jacket,** Adrian Mott; **Half-title page,** The Kobal Collection; **Title-page,** David Bailey; **p. 8** Horst; **p. 9** Cecil Beaton; **p. 10** (top) Toni Home Permanent; **p. 10** (below) Associated Press; **p. 12** G. Hoyningen-Huene, courtesy Horst; **pp. 13, 15, 16** Horst; **p. 19** Cecil Beaton; **p. 20** Associated Press; **p. 23** Horst; **p. 24** Popperfoto; **p. 25** Horst; **p. 26** Stanley Devon, courtesy *Sunday Times*; **p. 27** Norman Eales; **p. 28** Horst; **pp. 31, 35** Horst; **p. 36** Cecil Beaton; **p. 38** courtesy Betty Vacani; **p. 40** Hay Wrightson, courtesy John Cawthorne; **p. 41** Horst; **p. 44** Hay Wrightson, courtesy John Cawthorne; **p. 45** Houston Rogers, courtesy Mrs Niall; **pp. 46, 47** Lenare; **p. 48** Edington Vincent, courtesy Mrs Robert Morley; **p. 52** Radio Times Hulton Picture Library; **p. 53** Cecil Beaton; **p. 54** Manolo Blahnik; **p. 55** Baron de Meyer, courtesy Martin Battersby; **p. 57** (top and below right) Cecil Beaton; (below left) Horst; **p. 59** Helmut Newton; **p. 60** Cecil Beaton; **p. 61** John Timbers; **p. 63** Hay Wrightson, courtesy John Cawthorne; **p. 64** Helmut Newton; **p. 65** Tony Duffy, courtesy *Sunday Times*; **p. 66** Just Jacken, courtesy *Sunday Times*; **p. 67** Horst; **p. 69** Cecil Beaton; **p. 70** G. Hoyningen-Huene, courtesy Horst; **p. 71** Cecil Beaton; **p. 73** (top) Thames Television; (below) London Express News and Feature Service; **p. 74** The Kobal Collection; **p. 76** courtesy Max Factor; **pp. 77–89** The Kobal Collection; **p. 90** Terence Donovan; **p. 93** G. Hoyningen-Huene, courtesy Horst; **p. 95** Henri Cartier-Bresson/John Hillelson Agency; **p. 99** *Daily Mirror*; **p. 101** courtesy Mary Quant; **p. 102** courtesy Sarah Moon; **p. 103** (top) London Express News and Feature Service; (below) courtesy Barbara Hulanicki; **p. 104** Alfa Castaldi, courtesy Nanni Strada/Italian *Vogue*; **p. 105** (left) courtesy Barbara Hulanicki; (right) *Daily Mirror*; **pp. 106/7** Norman Eales; **p. 108** Henri Cartier-Bresson/John Hillelson Agency; **p. 111** Scaioni studio, courtesy Sir Norman Hartnell; **p. 112** courtesy Mrs Vera Poincin; **p. 113** courtesy Baroness d'Erlanger; **p. 115** Radio Times Hulton Picture Library; **pp. 116, 117** courtesy Christian Dior; **p. 118** Hatami, courtesy Yves St Laurent; **p. 119** courtesy Mrs Vera Poincin; **pp. 120, 122** J. F. Clair, courtesy *Elle*; **p. 123** courtesy *Elle*; **p. 124** courtesy Leslie Kark; **p. 125** Tommy Dixon/*Sunday Times*; **p. 126** courtesy Courrèges; **p. 129** courtesy Simone d'Aillencourt; **pp. 130, 131, 135** David Bailey; **p. 137** John French Library; **p. 138** G. Hoyningen-Huene, courtesy Horst; **p. 139** Man Ray, courtesy Lady Penrose; **p. 141** courtesy Revlon; **p. 142** courtesy Fabergé; **p. 143** (top), **144** (top) G. Hoyningen-Huene, courtesy Horst; **p. 143** (below), **144** (below) Horst; **p. 145** (top) John French Library; (below) Radio Times Hulton Picture Library; **p. 146** John French Library; **p. 147** David Bailey; **p. 148** (left) John French Library; (right) courtesy Leslie Kark; **pp. 149, 150, 151** (left) John French Library; **p. 151** (right) Associated News Group; **p. 152** David Bailey; **p. 154** (top) London Express News and Feature Service; (below) courtesy Neville Shulman; **p. 155** Barry Lategan; **p. 156** Patrick Hunt; **p. 157** David Bailey; **p. 158** Terence Donovan; **p. 159** Barry Lategan, courtesy Conde Nast; **p. 160** James Wedge, courtesy *Sunday Times*; **p. 161** Peter Knapp, courtesy *Sunday Times*; **p. 162** (top) courtesy Bob Wright for Dunn-Meynell Keefe; (below) Colin Jones, courtesy *Sunday Times*; **p. 164** Keystone Press; **p. 165** William Claxton; **p. 166** (left) courtesy Yves St Laurent; (right) courtesy Annie Walker; **p. 167** Syndication International; **p. 168** courtesy Fisons Chemicals; **p. 169** (top) courtesy Contemporary Films; (below) Syndication International; **pp. 170/1** Norman Eales; **p. 172** John Timbers; **p. 173** Radio Times Hulton Picture Library; **p. 174** David Montgomery; **p. 175** (top) Kelvin Brodie, courtesy *Sunday Times*; **pp. 176, 177** Pat Booth; **p. 178** United Press International; **p. 179** Peter Knapp, courtesy *Sunday Times*; **pp. 180/1** Harri Peccinotti; **p. 182** Peter Knapp, courtesy *Sunday Times*; **p. 184** courtesy Ponds; **pp. 186/7** courtesy National Dairy Council/Robert Updegraff; **pp. 188/9** Norman Parkinson, courtesy Mark Boxer; **p. 191** Reprinted from Seventeen Magazine © 1953 Triangle Communications Inc. (All rights reserved) photograph by Dan Wynn; **pp. 192, 193** courtesy Revlon; **p. 194** Norman Parkinson/Adrian Mott, courtesy *Harpers-Queen*; **p. 195** Paul Huf; **pp. 196, 197** Terence Donovan; **pp. 198/9** John Timbers; **pp. 200, 201, 202** courtesy Adel Rootstein; **p. 203** courtesy Lester Gaba; **p. 204** courtesy *Elle*; **p. 207** Camera Press; **p. 208** courtesy Patrick Hunt; **p. 209** Ronald Traeger; **pp. 210, 211** Harri Peccinotti; **pp. 212, 213** (top) David Bailey; (below) Valerie Santiago; **p. 214** Pelito for *Sunday Times*; **p. 215** Painting by Augustus John, courtesy National Museum of Wales; **p. 216** Harri Peccinotti; **p. 218, 219** Maureen Lambray, courtesy Caterine Milinaire; **p. 220** Adrian Mott.